Skateboarding:

Book of Tricks

Andy Gluszko

The Silver Strand Crew 7-03

Skateboarding:
Book of Tricks

Steve Badillo
Doug Werner

Tracks Publishing
San Diego, California

Photography by
Ariel Shaw
Mikey Pacheco
Steve Badillo
Doug Werner
Mike Franklin

All tricks performed by Steve Badillo
unless otherwise noted

Mikey Pacheco

Skateboarding: Book of Tricks

Steve Badillo / Doug Werner

Tracks Publishing
140 Brightwood Avenue
Chula Vista, CA 91910
619-476-7125
tracks@cox.net
www.startupsports.com

Second Printing 8-04

Publisher's Cataloging-in-Publication

Badillo, Steve.
Skateboarding : book of tricks / Steve Badillo, Doug Werner ; photography by Ariel Shaw ... [et al.].
p. cm.
Includes index.
Audience: Ages 10-25.
LCCN 2003110892
ISBN 1-884654-19-3

1. Skateboarding. I. Werner, Doug, 1950- II. Title.

GV859.8.B33 2003 796.22
QBI03-200658

This book is dedicated to the people who design, build and finance skateparks. Without them skateboarders would not have playgrounds to grow up in. Lush forests provide a place for animals and go through a rebirth when fire burns down the trees — new life springs from ashes. So it is when skateparks are built then torn down and then built again. They provide a place for the growing skateboarder. New terrain will always encourage those who skate.

Ariel Shaw

Steve Badillo and Ariel Shaw

Doug Werner

Acknowledgements

Skatelab
Camarillo Boys and Girls Club
Silver Strand
Todd Huber
Scott Radinsky
Becca Badillo
Gavin Badillo
Brahyan Lopez
Simon Corral
Torey Pudwill
Ariel Shaw
Mikey Pacheco
Mike Franklin
Daniel Sabelis
Aisha Buxton
Phyllis Carter
Andy Gluszko
Joey Gluszko

And thanks to these companies
Alva Skateboards
DVS shoes
Fury Trucks
Go Urethane Wheels
Lance Mountain and The Firm

Special thanks to

Riders Tory Pudwill, Brahyan Lopez and Simon Corral

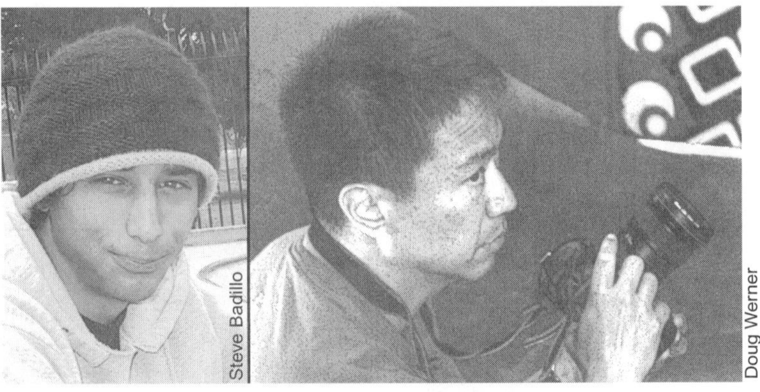

Photographers Mikey Pacheco and Ariel Shaw

Todd Huber
Skatelab Skatepark
and Museum

Mikey Pacheco

Preface

Book of Tricks was written to show my old-school and new-school skateboarding influences. I'm not saying that one is better then the other, but that skateboarders need both old school and new school to be well-rounded. Tricks presented here are not the only kinds of old-school and new-school skateboarding — this book shows my style of old school and new school.

I emphasize the importance of being able to transfer from one ramp to another as a way to adapt to different types of skateboarding terrains. Make skateboarding what you want it to be, and you will be satisfied with your efforts.

Have fun with skateboarding and learn a new trick.

Sk8 Tuff. Steve

Warning label
Skateboarding can be dangerous. Riders should know and follow safe skateboarding procedures at all times and wear appropriate safety gear.
Mikey Pacheco

Contents

rider: Torey Pudwill

Steve Badillo

Doug Werner

Steve Badillo

1

old school

Mikey Pacheco

Doug Werner

Old school

I learned most of these old-school tricks in the mid- to late '80s — back when riding jump ramps, skating ditches and building backyard halfpipes were the thing to do. There were only a few skateparks around so we had to build our own ramps.

My influences back then were the original Bones Brigade Team (Lance Mountain, Steve Caballero and Tony Hawk), Christian Hosoi and Mark Gonzales. Tricks shown here can be traced to these legendary skaters. I'm stoked I was skateboarding when professional skateboarding was so young. I idolized these guys when I was a kid. They made skateboarding fun. The old-school style will always be a part of skateboarding and its roots.

frontside boneless

Doug Werner

Ariel Shaw / sequence

The boneless was probably one of the first tricks I learned when I was a kid. You can bust out a boneless almost anywhere — ramps, banks, bowls, flat ground, curbs. Approach the bank with medium speed. Bend your knees and reach down with your Indy hand and grab the board. When you get to the top of the bank, plant your front foot and pop the nose up with your tail foot and Indy hand. Pull the board up and out to extend your tail foot for

full extension. Then with your plant foot, jump up and start to bring the nose around 180. Bring your plant foot back on the board in the air as you start to land on the bank. Let go of the board and lean forward as you ride down the bank. Make sure your feet are on the bolts for stability. Stoked. Now try a frontside 360 boneless.

SKATELAB
EXIT
OSIRIS
8
9

backside boneless

Doug Werner

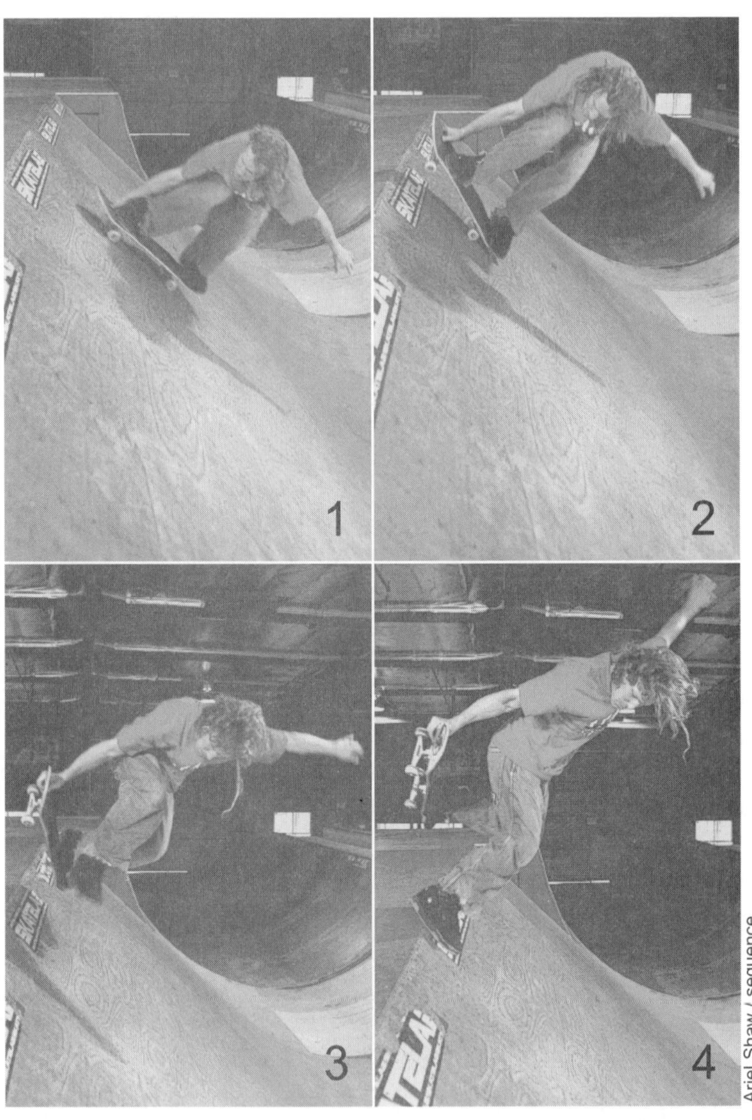

Ariel Shaw / sequence

This trick is timeless. Old pro vert riders, such as Jeff Phillips, do it the best. Like the frontside boneless, this trick can be done on almost any terrain. Ride up the bank with medium speed. Bend your knees and reach down with your backside grab hand (lead hand behind your front foot). When you grab the board pop the nose up with your tail foot. Air the board up as you start to plant your front foot on the bank. With your front foot planted, extend

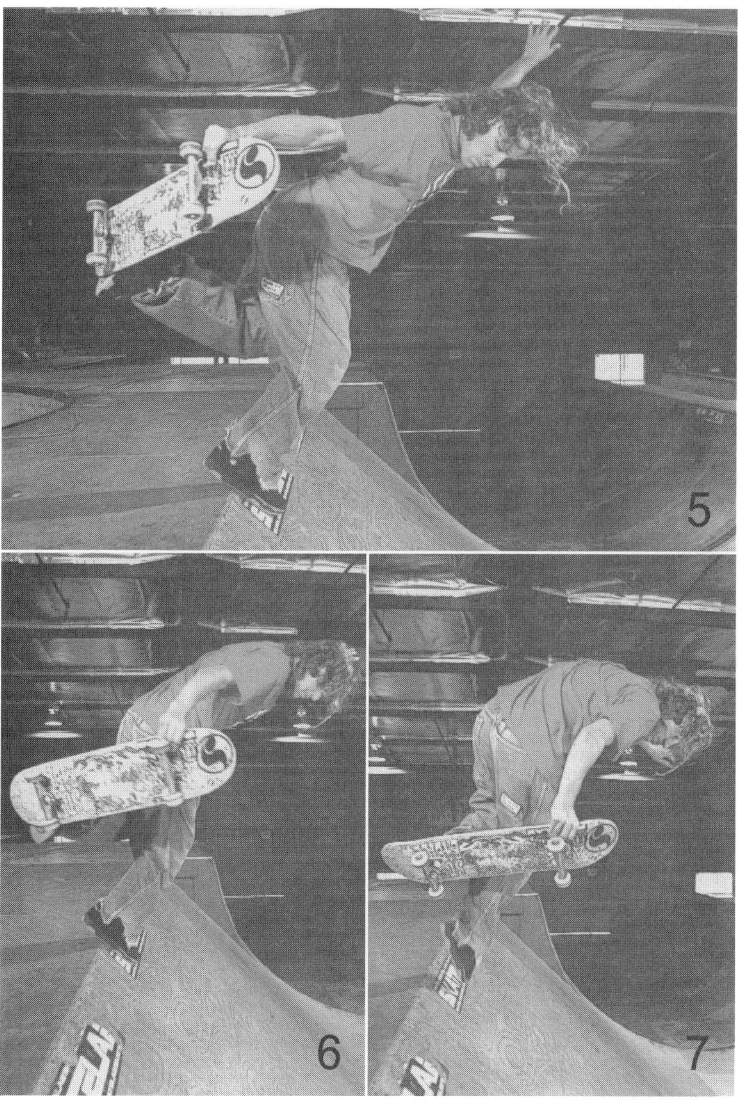

your tail foot out and around. Full extension will help you land this trick. Now jump up with your planted foot and start to bring the nose of the board around and under your feet. Let go of the board and lean forward as you ride down the bank. Make sure your feet are on the bolts for stability. Cool old school.

8
9
10

Mikey Pacheco

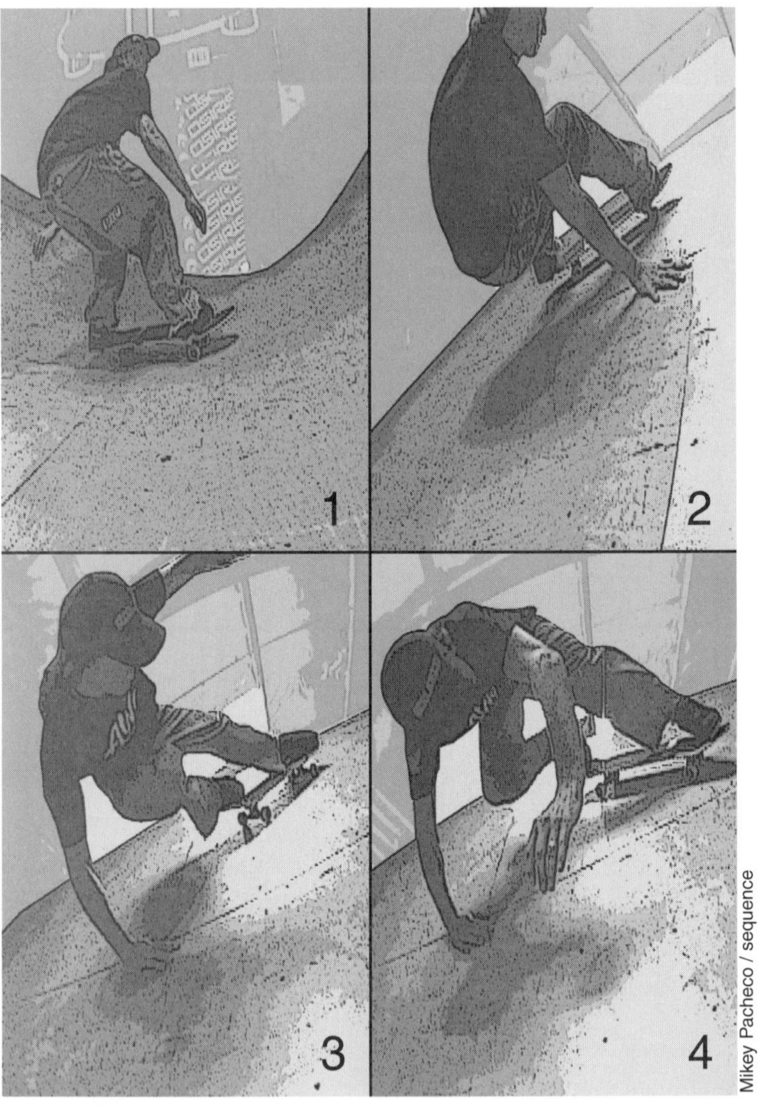

Mikey Pacheco / sequence

The Bertslide was named for the influential surfer Larry Bertleman. This slide can be done on flat ground or banks. Ride toward the bank or flat ground with enough speed to help you rotate the board. As you approach the bank lay down your lead hand on the bank while you start to slide your tail foot frontside. Extend your legs out and around as you over-rotate the slide.

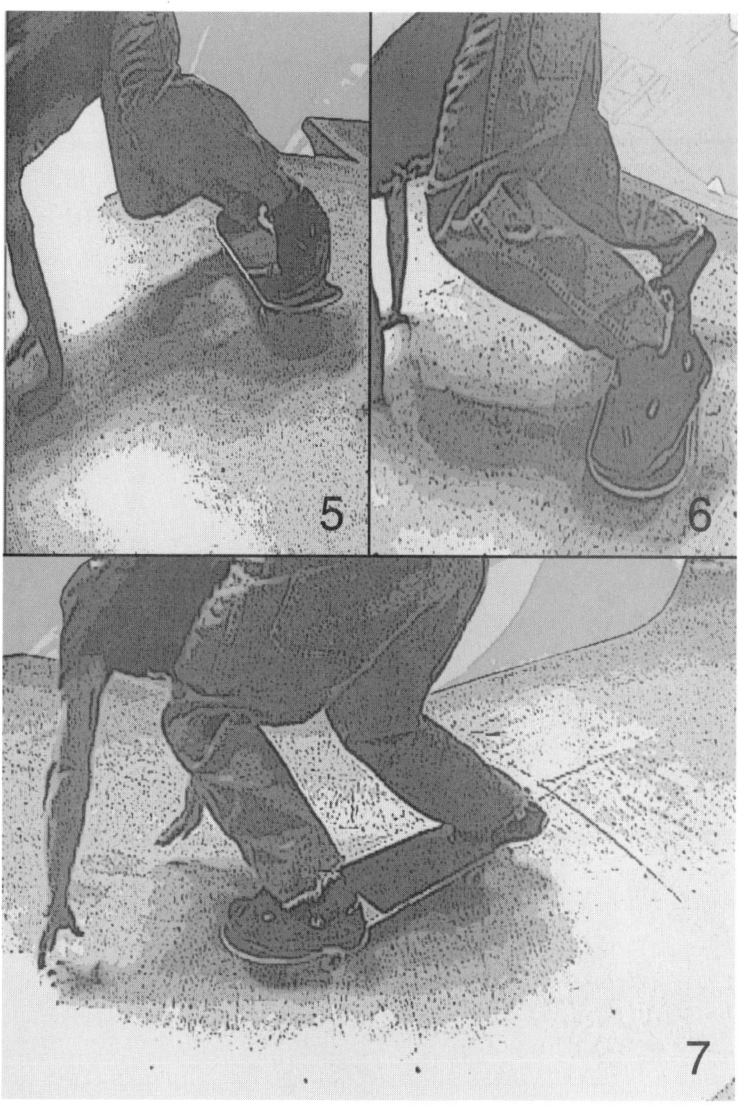

When the board comes around 360, put your trailing hand down to help you slide the last 180. Push off the bank with your hands as you bring the nose around 540. Ride away feeling good. Now try a backside 540 slide.

8

madonna

Doug Werner

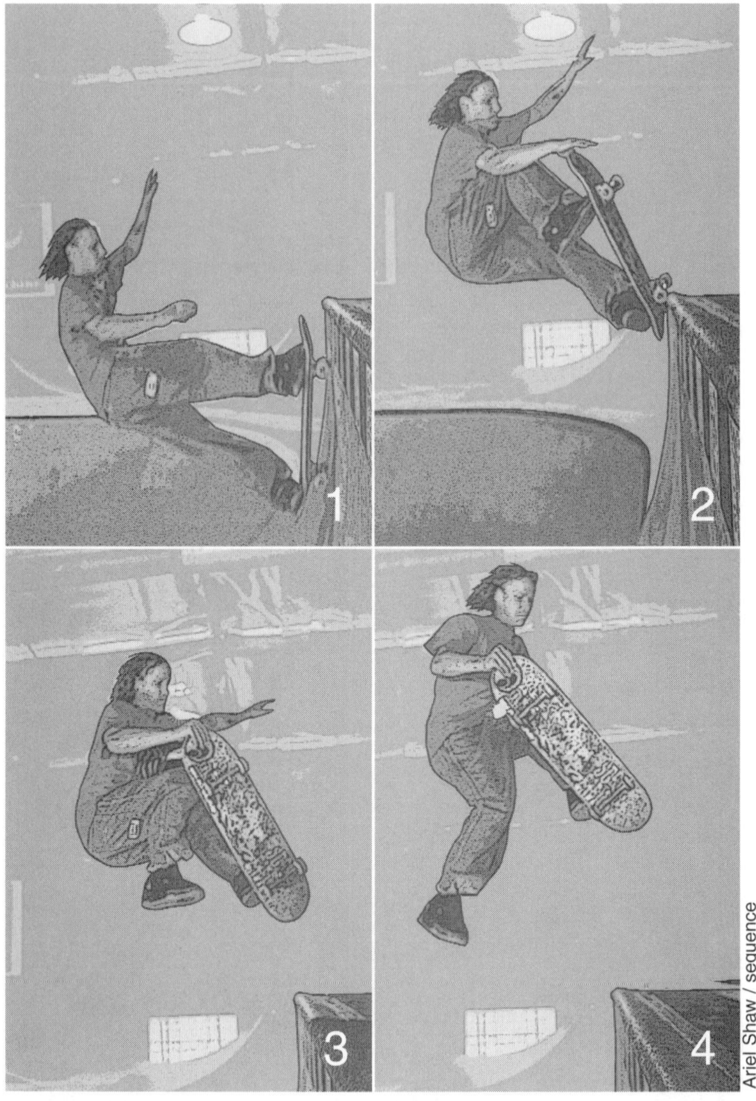

Ariel Shaw / sequence

Madonna did not invent this trick. Do this trick on the biggest ramp you can find. Get as much speed as you possibly can and ride straight up the transition. When you get to the coping, float an air as you grab the nose with your lead hand. Start to float frontside as you take your front foot off the board and kick it out straight down (full extension). Now try to slap your tail to the

5
6
7

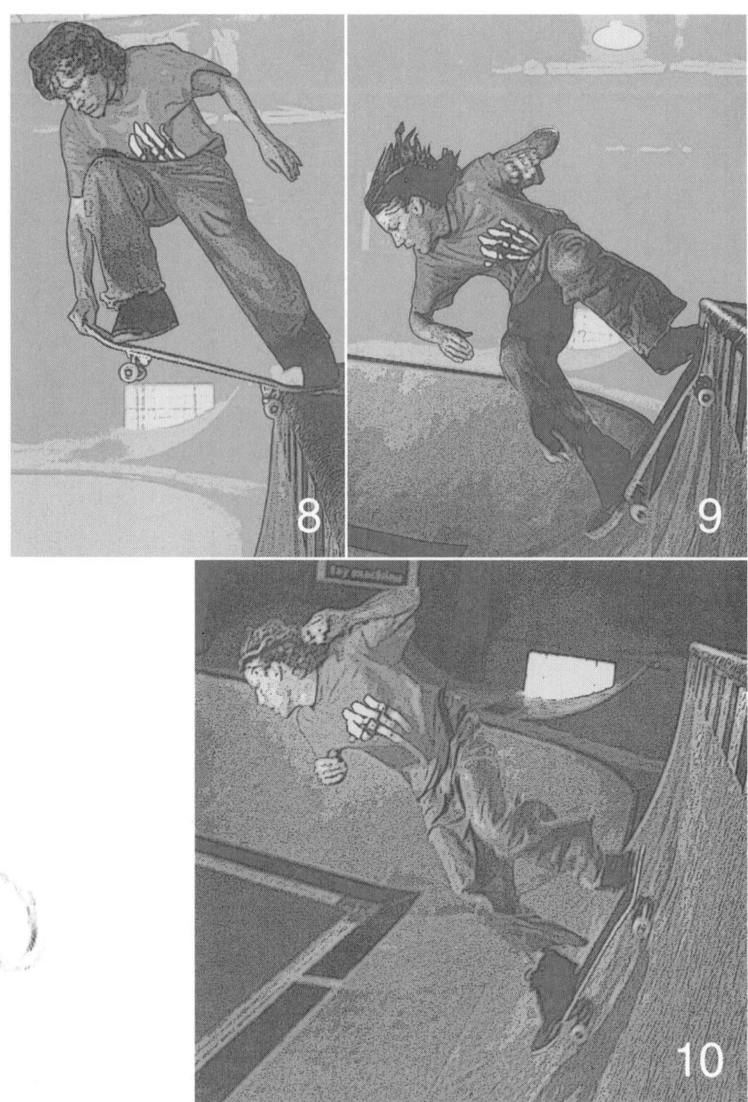

coping as you bring your front foot back on the board. Once you slap your tail down, lean forward as you drop in and ride away with the song, "Like a Virgin," on your mind.

no comply

Doug Werner

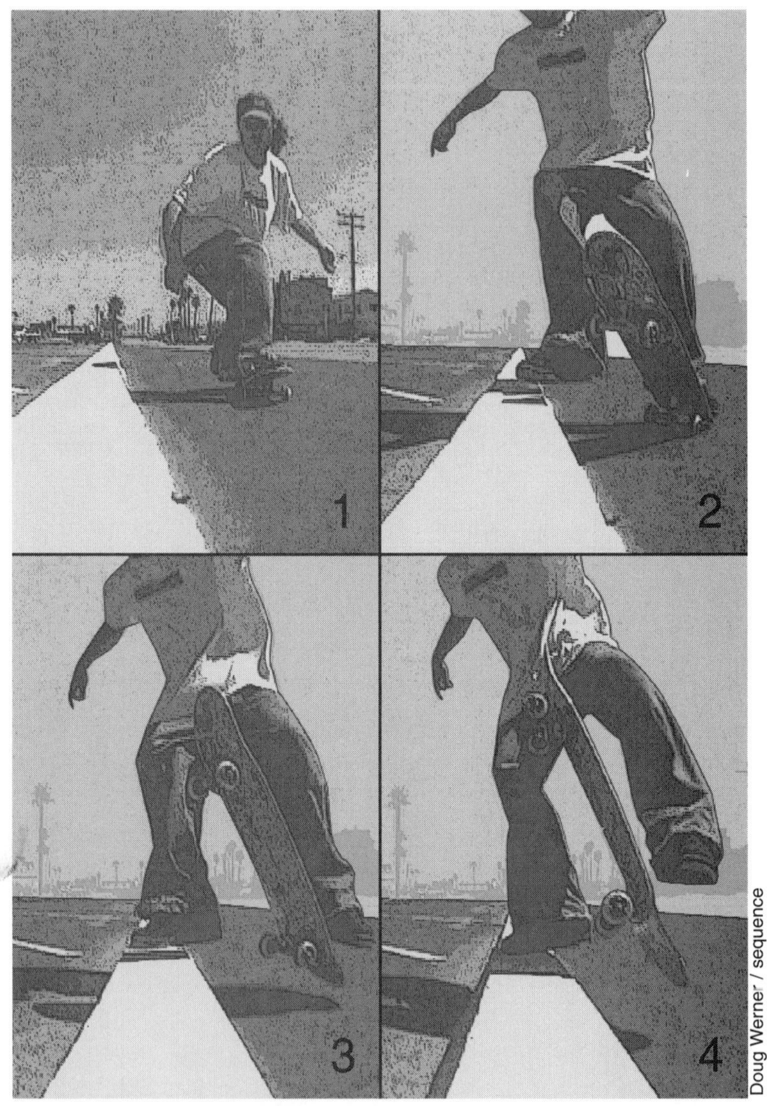

Doug Werner / sequence

You can do this trick anywhere on any terrain at any time — even in your sleep. With medium speed plant your front foot down as you start to snap the tail and bring the board around frontside. Kick your tail foot out and around 180. The board will follow your back leg. Jump off the ground with your front foot and land back on the board. You should be riding fakie at this

point. After you land this trick a few times, try to do it 360. Just over-rotate the no comply frontside 360.

8
9
10

Doug Werner

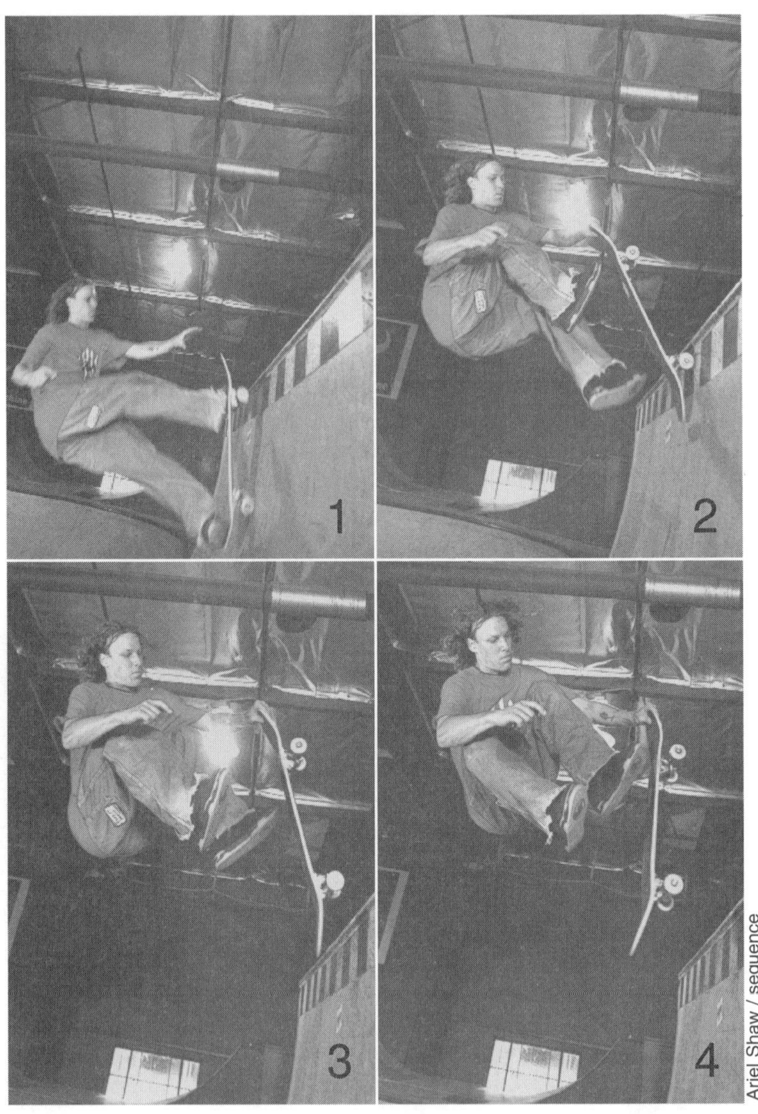

Ariel Shaw / sequence

Not seen that often and that's what makes it a gem. The bigger the ramp the easier it is to pull off. Ride straight up the ramp with full speed. As you pop off the coping reach and grab the nose with your trailing hand (tail hand). In the air you are going to suck up your knees to your chest and do the body variel part. Switch your feet in the air so the start of the trick is a nose grab

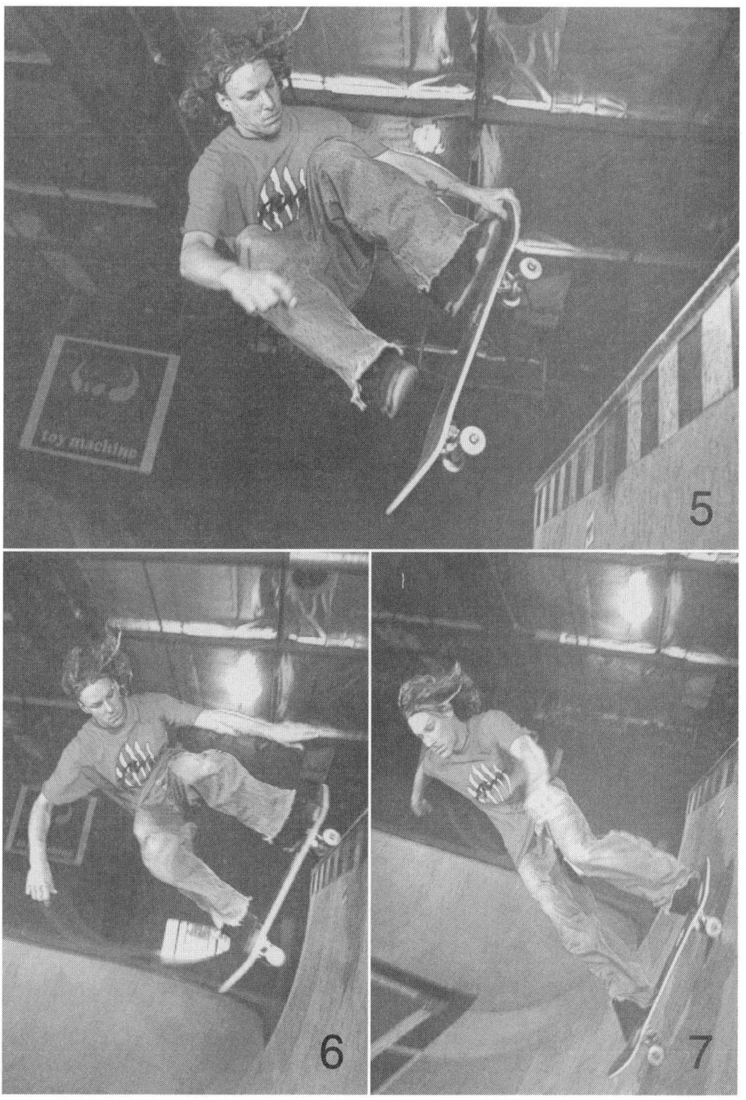

and ends up as a tail grab. Spread your feet out as you start to land the trick. Let go of the board and ride down the transitions. Do it again. It feels good.

8

frigit air

Mikey Pacheco

One of my favorite tricks. I have been doing this trick since the California Amateur Skateboard League (CASL) used it as a logo for their contests way back in the mid-'80s. This trick can be done on jump ramps, banks and ramps. Approach the lip with full speed and ollie forward as you grab the nose with your lead hand. Then start to kick out your front foot in the frigit position. Lean forward in the air and when you start to come down, bring your foot back to the top of the board. Let go and lean forward as you land it. Cool. Now go join CASL.

Mikey Pacheco / sequence

5
6
7

8
9

judo air

Doug Werner

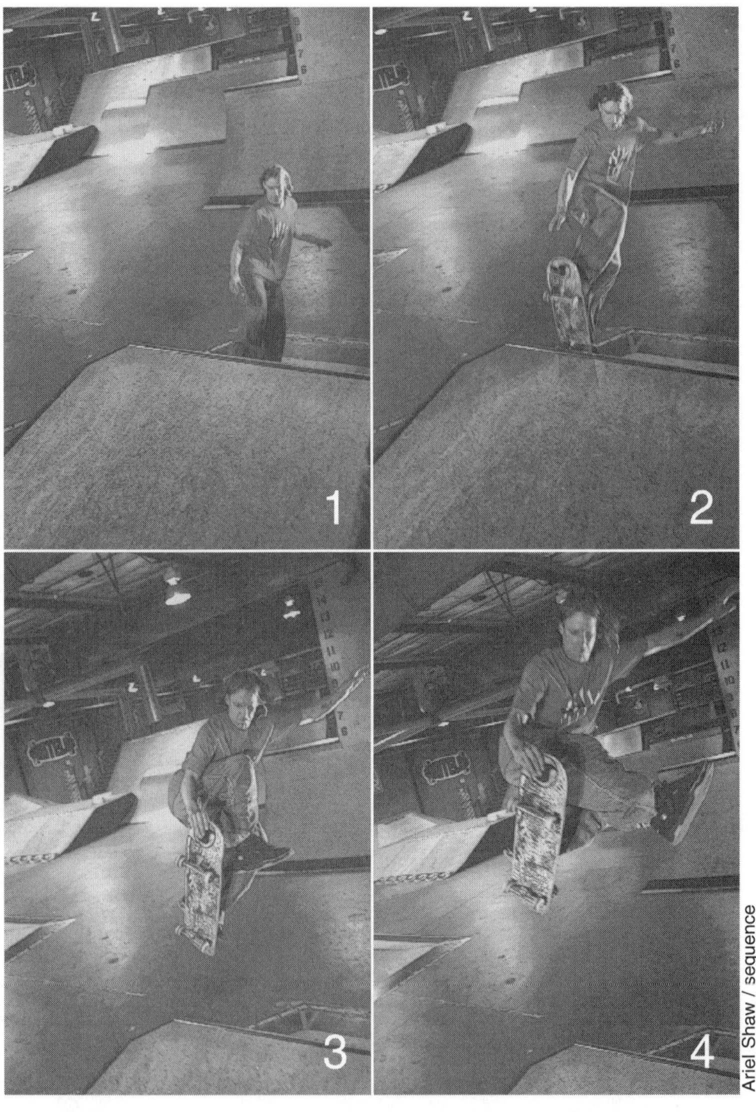

Ariel Shaw / sequence

This is the exact opposite of the frigit air. It's called the judo air because you can kick someone in the face if they are not watching. It can be done on jump ramps, banks and ramps. Ride up the transitions with as much speed as possible. Then ollie off the top of the lip and grab the nose with your lead hand. Start to kick out your front foot in the judo position. Stall it in the air as

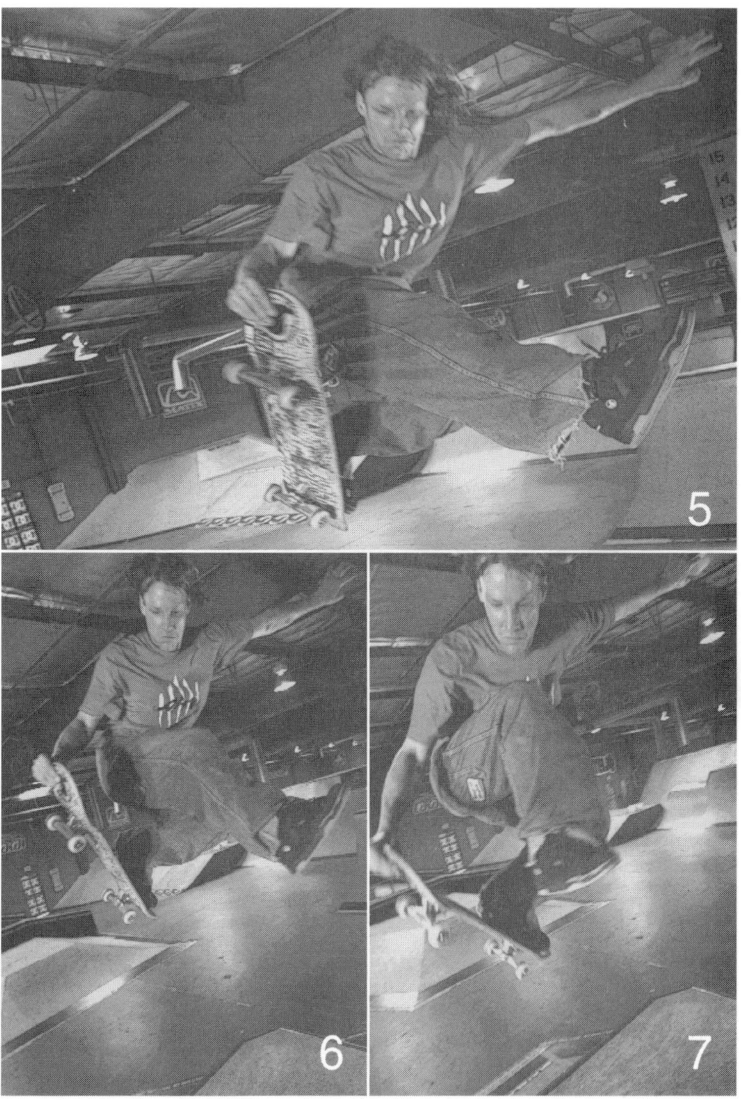

long as possible. Bring your foot back to the top of the board as you lean forward. Let go of the board and land it. Now try a judo frigit air.

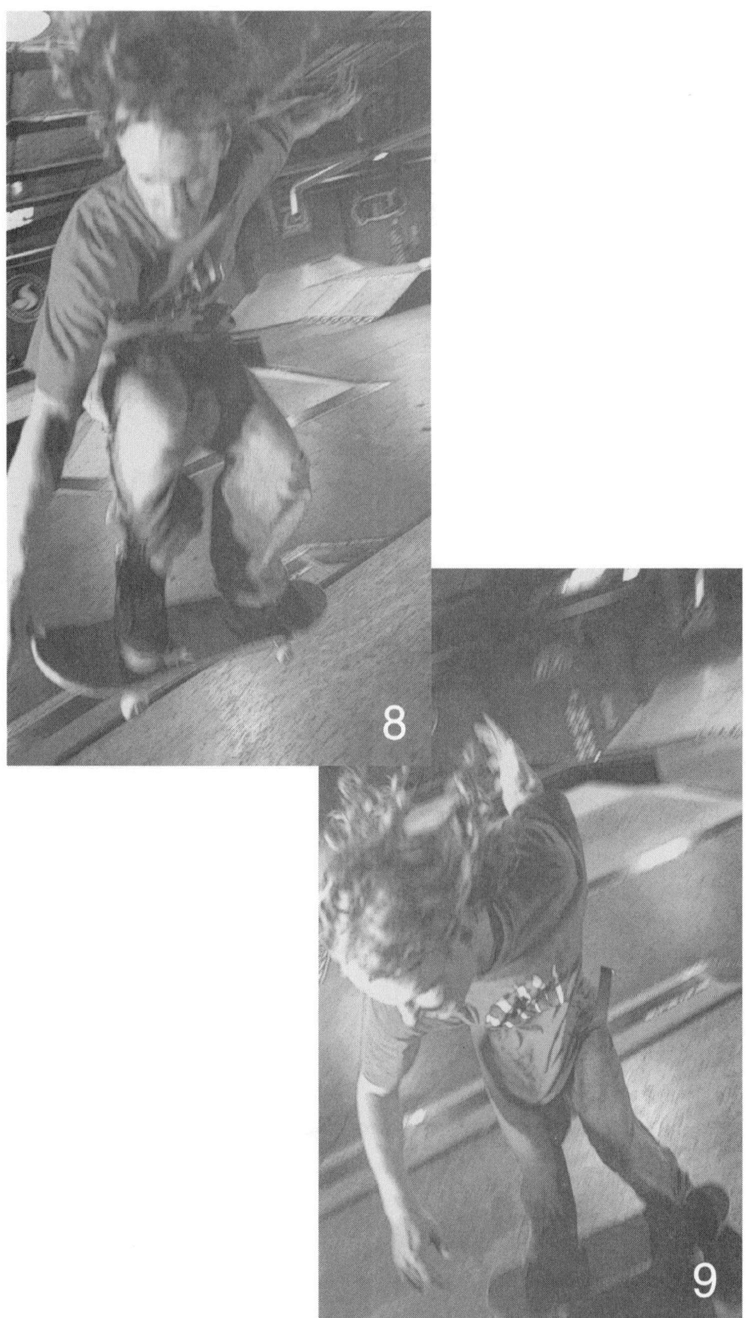
8
9

Doug Werner

Ariel Shaw / sequence

After learning judos and frigits, the next trick for you is a combination of both. With full speed launch off the ramp. Grab the nose with your lead hand and kick out your front foot in the judo position. At the same time kick out your tail foot in the frigit position. This is the airwalk position. Extend and stall this air as long as possible. Your board should be away from your feet. As you

start to come down, pull your feet back to their original position on top of the bolts. Let go of the board and ride away leaning forward. Then try a finger flip airwalk.

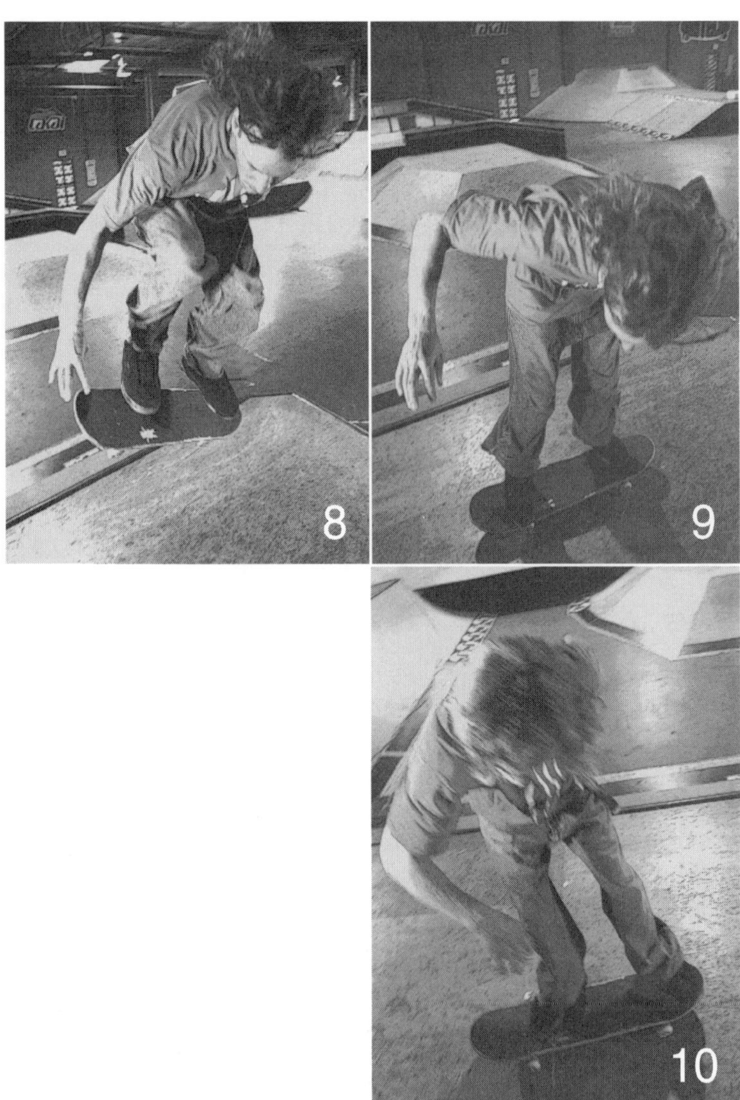
8
9
10

backside
180 variel

Mikey Pacheco

Mikey Pacheco / sequence

Whenever you do an air and land fakie, it's a leap of faith. Try to know you are going to land it. Ride up to the coping with mucho speed. When you hit the lip, start rotating backside. Spin the board backside with your feet as you grab with your lead hand. Grab the board in the middle. Keep rotating your shoulders and waist 180 and variel the board under your feet. Spread your feet

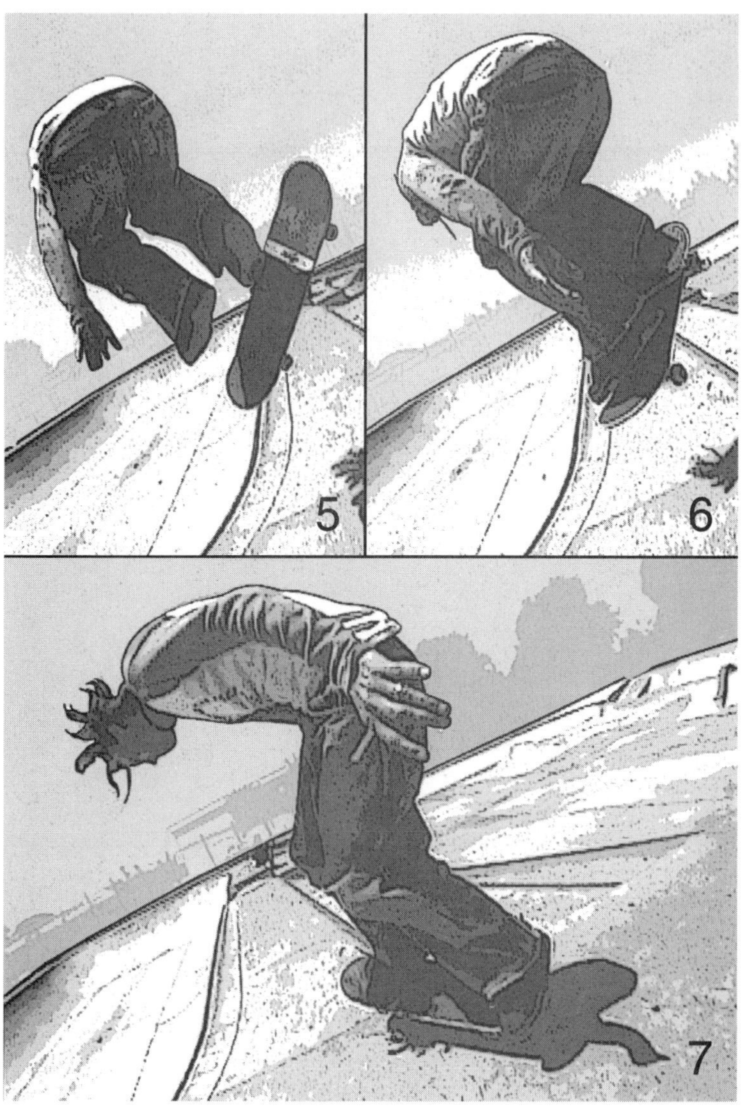

out over the bolts as you start to land it. When you land, lean fakie and throw your arms in the air. Remember, the faster you go, the higher you go and the more time you have to variel the board around.

8
9

layback
grind
revert
Mikey Pacheco

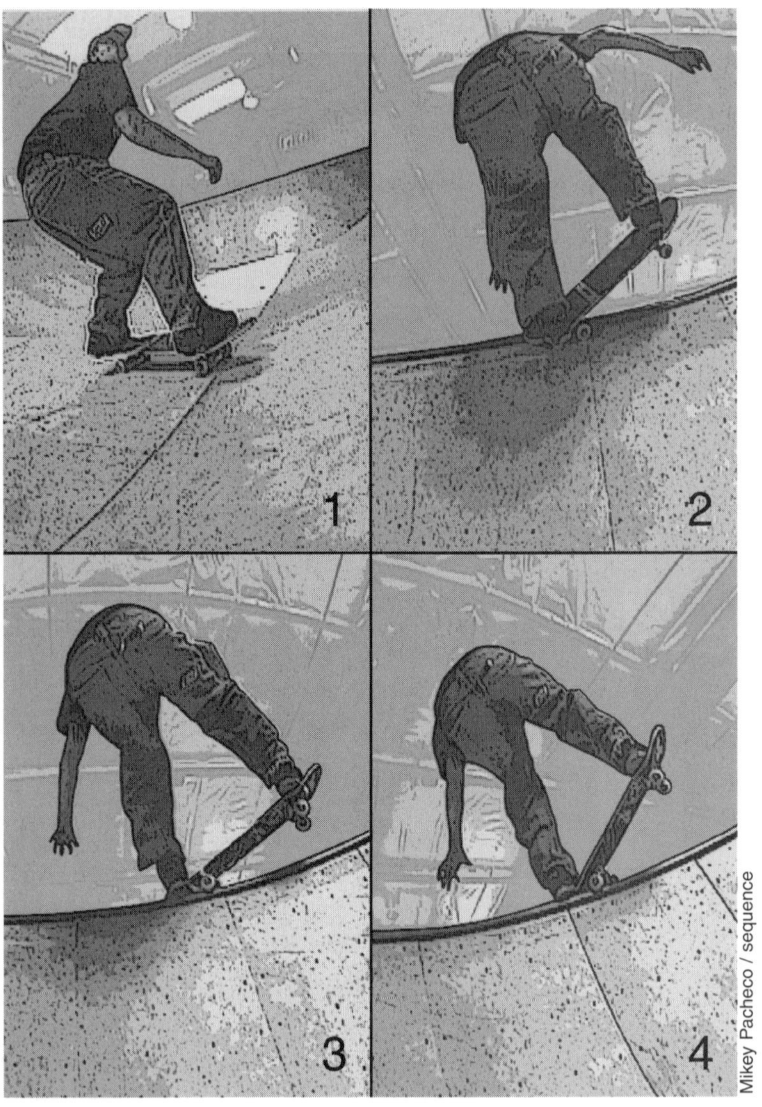

Mikey Pacheco / sequence

My favorite skater to do this trick was an Alva Boy — Bill Danforth. This trick can be done in bowls, pools and ramps. Ride up the ramp going frontside with medium to fast speed. Start carving frontside and grind into a 5-0 grind. Bend your knees and with your trailing hand reach down and behind for the coping. As you grind frontside grab the coping and push your tail

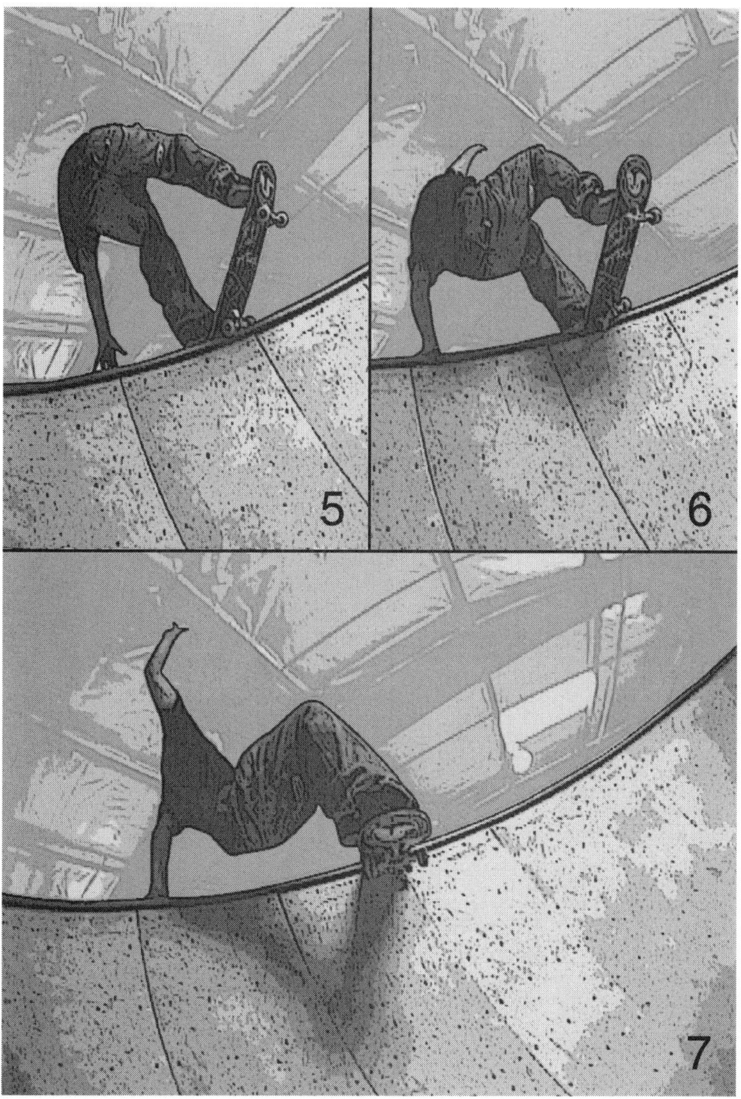

foot out to extend the layback grind. After you can layback no more go to tail and start to revert. To do this push the tail around 180 while you turn your waist and shoulders frontside. Come in fakie and lean that way. Skate away feeling like the "Nomad."

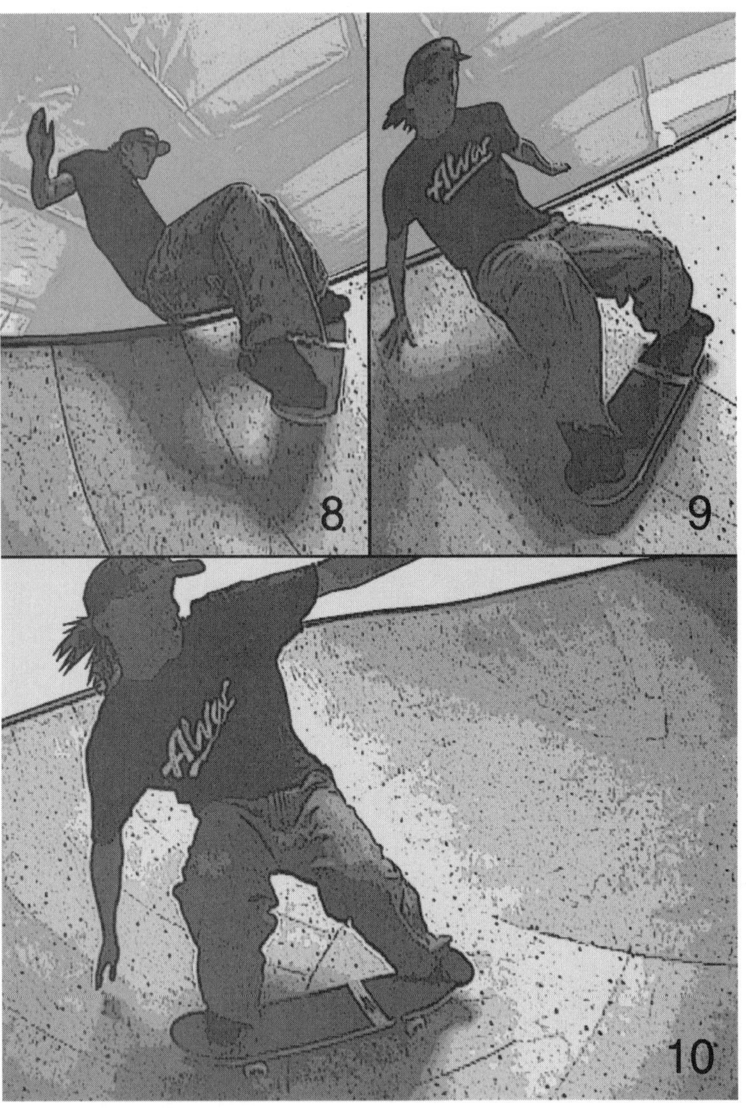
8
9
10

chapter one

sweeper

Mikey Pacheco

Mikey Pacheco / sequence

There are many variations of this trick, but this is the basic sweeper. This trick is done on banks and ramps. Ride up the ramp with just enough speed to get to the top. When you pop off the coping, grab the nose with your lead hand. As you grab, you should plant your tail foot on the coping. Start swinging frontside as you sweep the board across the deck of the ramp. Lay the tail

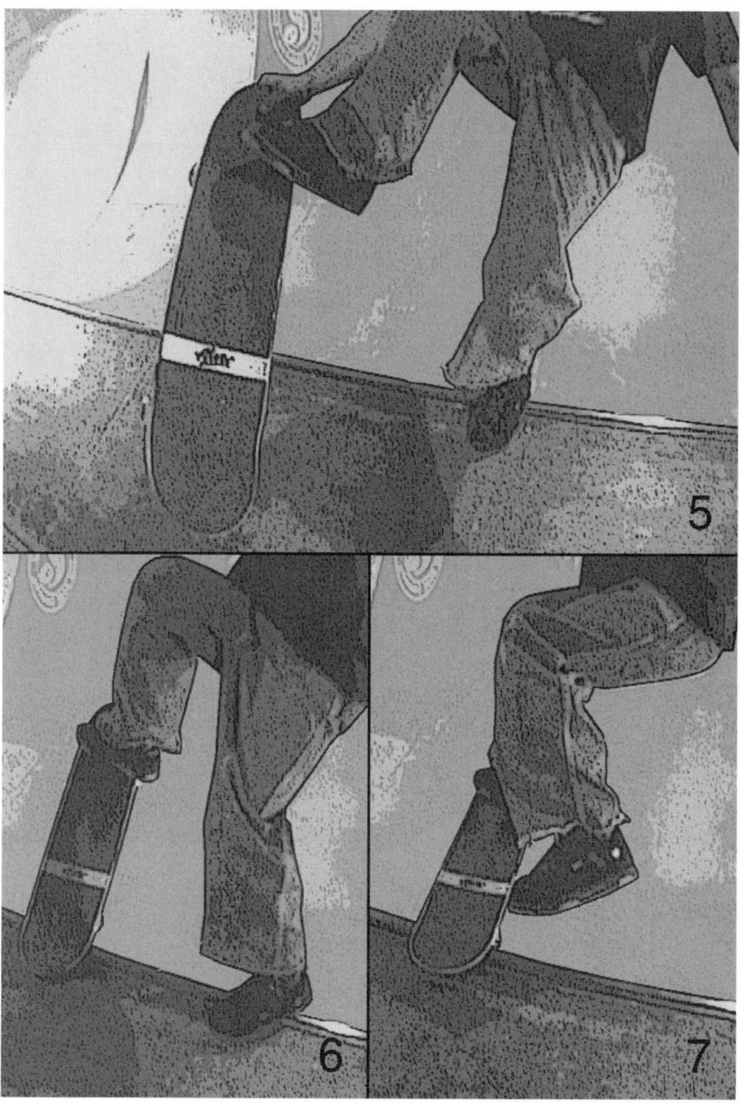

on the coping to drop back in. As you lay the tail down, jump back on it with your planted tail foot and lean forward. Let go of the board and ride to the other side. Now try it with the crail grab hand.

8
9

rocket air

Mikey Pacheco

Mikey Pacheco / sequence

Can you guess who invented this trick? You are right! Christian Hosoi — Mister High Air Hollywood himself. Skate as fast as you can toward your favorite jump ramp. Ollie big as you hit the coping. Grab the nose with both hands and start to drop your front foot down the board to the tail. Straighten out your legs and stall it out. When you start to land, pull your front foot back up

the board to the bolts and lean forward. Let go of the board and skate down the street. Now try Christian's 13-foot backside method air on a vert ramp.

old school

caballerial stall

Doug Werner

Ariel Shaw / sequence

All props go to the legend Steve Caballero for everything he has done for skateboarding and for inventing this trick. He is a true professional skateboarder. Start this trick going fakie with plenty of speed. Wind up your shoulders because you are going to spin 270. As you approach the coping, do a fakie ollie 270. Keep the rotation tight and near the coping. Lock your back truck onto the

coping as you are spinning. Then lay down your front truck on the coping. Now you are in the axle stall part. From there bring your nose around into the transition another 90 degrees. Lean forward and ride down the tranny while thinking about Stevie Caballero.

8
9

halfcab frontside rocknroll

Doug Werner

Ariel Shaw / sequence

This is a trick with STYLE. First learn to do normal frontside rocknrolls. Start out riding fakie. When your back truck gets close to the coping, start your halfcab. Bring the nose around 180. Point your front foot forward and twist your shoulders and waist toward the transitions. Look down into the transitions to help swing the board around frontside rocknroll. Stay centered over the board and ride it out. Styley.

POWELL
4

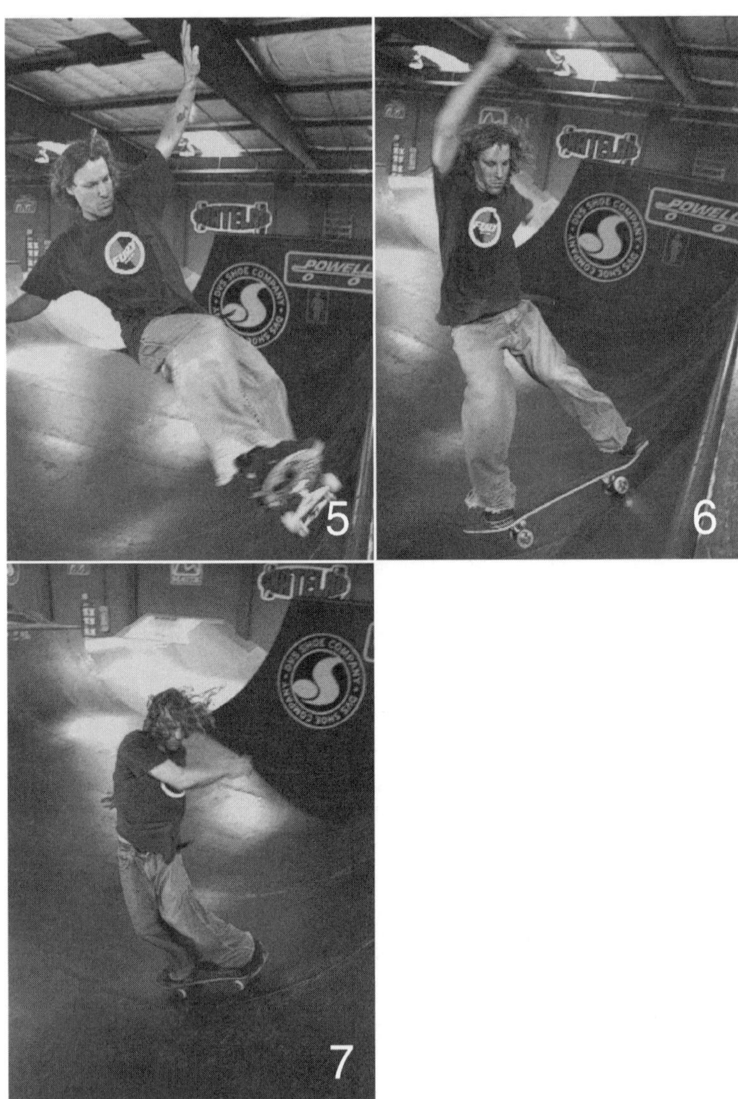
5
6
7
POWELL
DVS SHOE COMPANY

chapter one

backside variel disaster

Mike Franklin

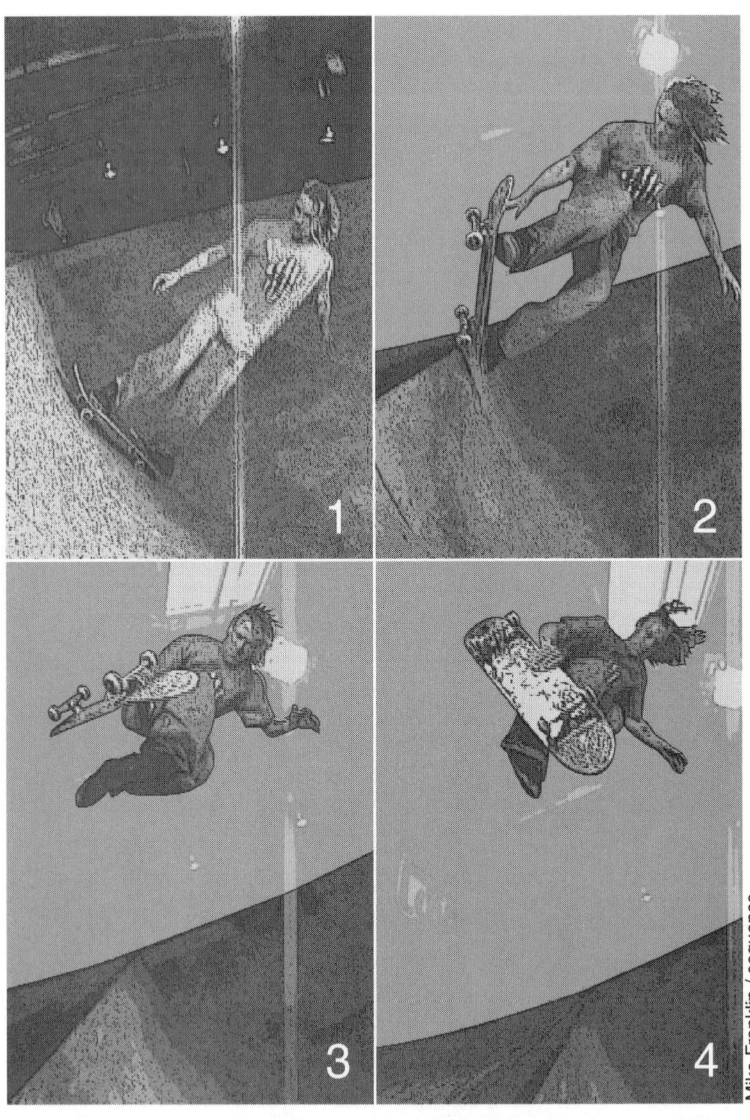

Mike Franklin / sequence

Tony Hawk invented this trick along with hundreds of others. Find a big ramp — it's easier on bigger ramps. You have to go Mach 5 when you reach the coping. As you hit it, shuvit the board with your feet and grab the board with your lead hand. Go as high as you can and variel the board under your feet. Try to spread your feet out over the bolts. Keep your head and body in

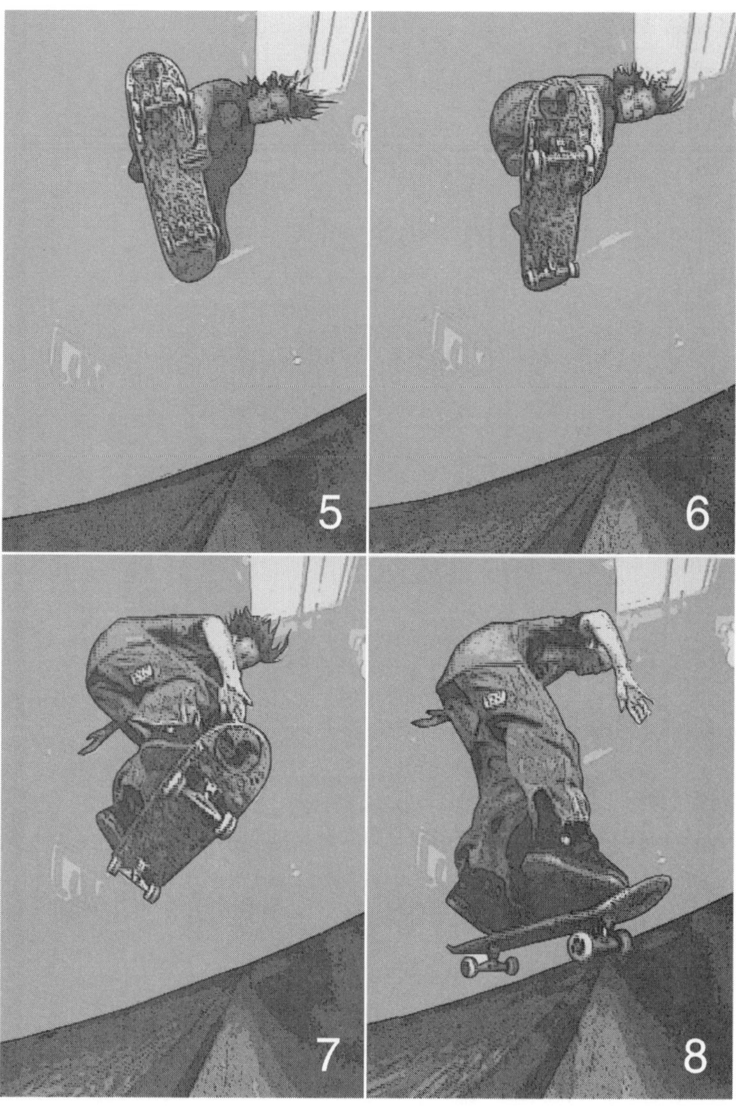

the transition to keep you centered. Land disaster and lean forward back into the tranny. Ride away feeling like Tony Hawk. Now go try his 900.

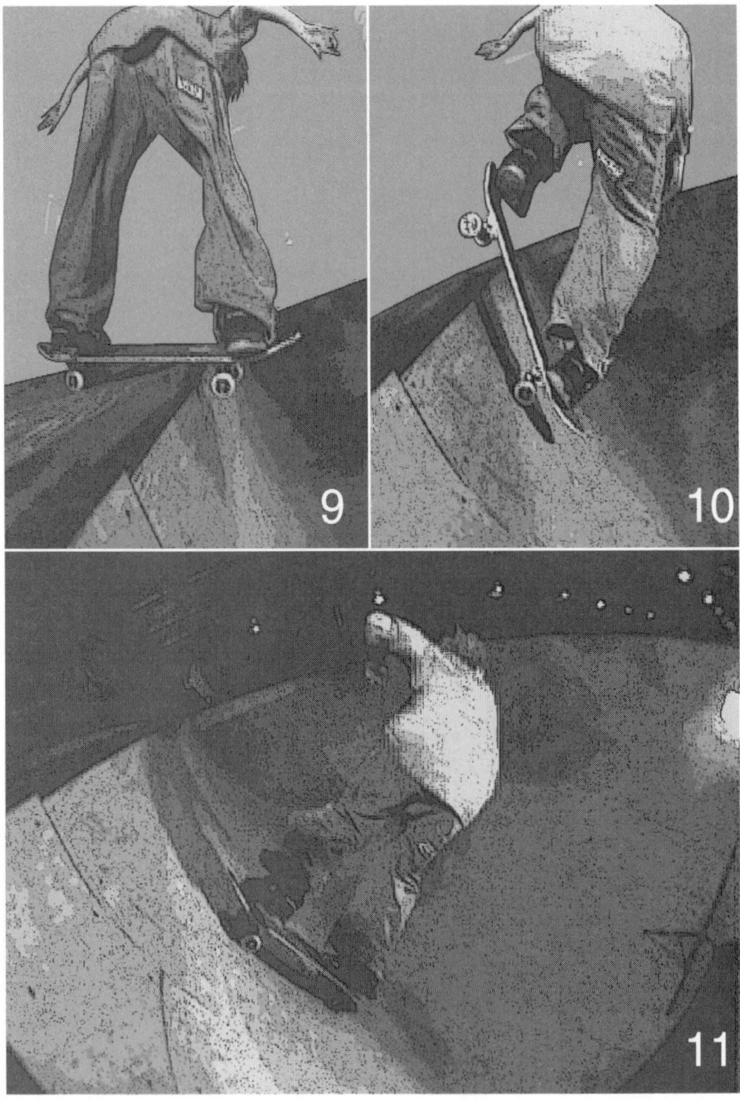
9
10
11

frontside variel air:
tale of a broken board

Mikey Pacheco

Variel airs can be done both ways. This is frontside. Learn it. Skate as fast as you can and ollie off the coping. With your lead hand, grab the board in the mute position in the middle of the board.

Mikey Pacheco / sequence

Start rotating the board frontside, but keep the board under your feet. Spread your feet over the bolts. If you have done it right, you will be holding the board backside. Lean forward as you start to land it. Let go of the board and ride away with another trick in your bag.Try not to break the board.

8

9

2

spine tricks

Doug Werner

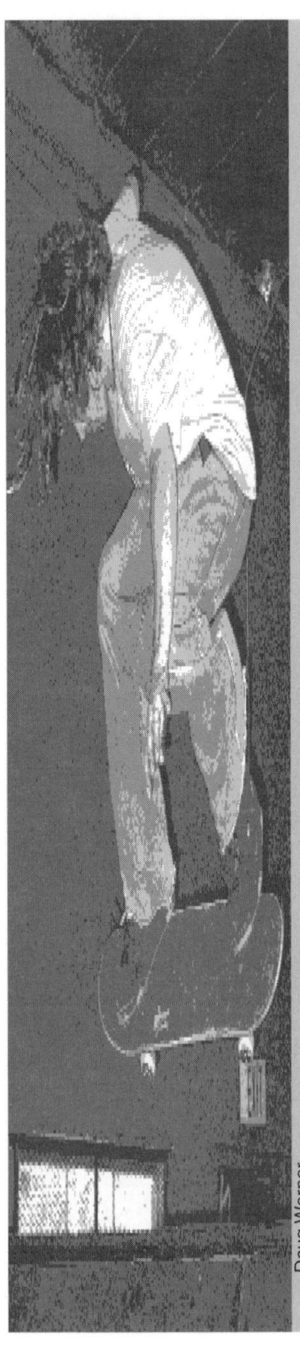

Doug Werner

Spine tricks

Spine ramps are one of my favorite terrains to skateboard. There are many different spine tricks that I like to skate, but here are three I think you will enjoy.

Spine ramps help you learn how to transfer from one transition to another. When spines are built farther away from each other, or from transition to bank, they make you want to use airs to transfer.

Nowadays most skateparks have spine ramps or transfers from one ramp to another. When you learn to transfer in and out of transitions, it helps you adapt to the terrain faster. Being able to transfer from ramp to ramp should be a staple in the modern skateboarder's bag of tricks.

Doug Werner

Ariel Shaw / sequence

I learned this trick in 1989 when I saw a sequence of it in *Thrasher*. I have been doing it ever since. Ride up the transitions going frontside with a fair amount of speed. Start hitting the angle frontside into the grind. It helps to grind 5-0 first, then point your front foot down into the smith position. As you are grinding smith, start leaning with your waist and head into the

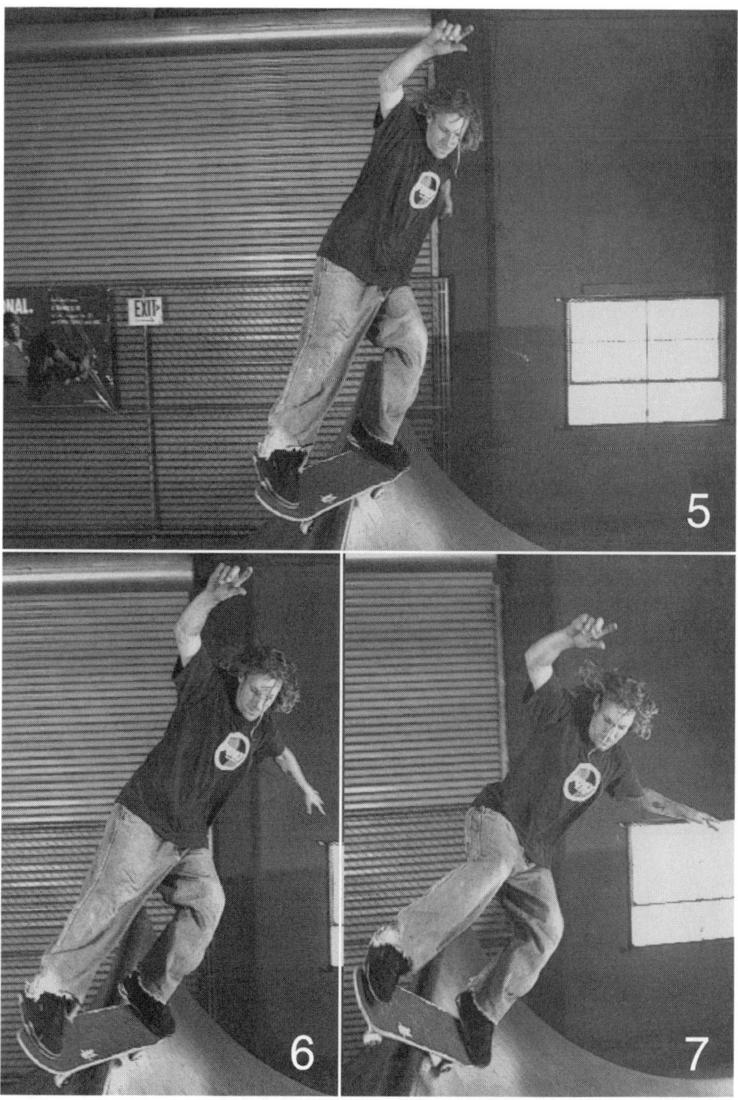

fakie position so your smith grind turns into a feeble grind. Grind as long as possible to give you more time to lean into the fakie position. Then start coming back in fakie and ride it out.

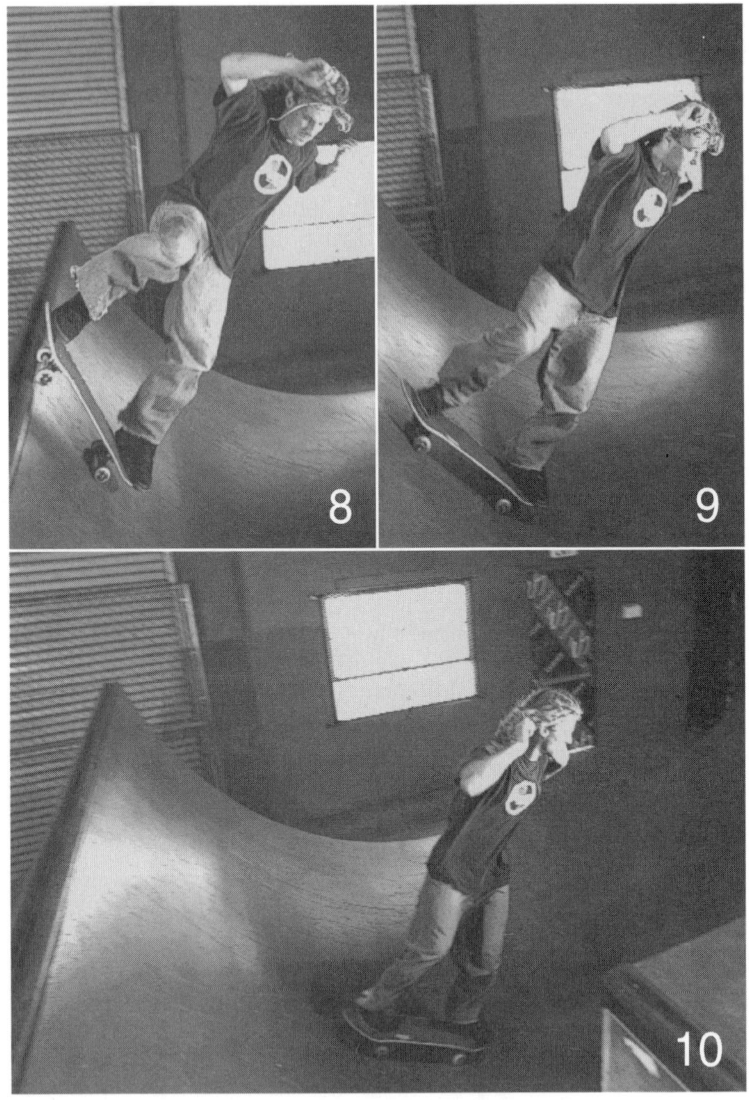
8
9
10

fakie pivot grind over spine
EXIT
Doug Werner

Ariel Shaw / sequence

John Cardiel does the best fakie pivot grinds. He does them fast, smooth and with style. First you have to start out going fakie with a lot of speed to carry you through the trick. Hit the angle just before you start grinding the coping. Aim your back truck, which is really your front truck in this trick, for the coping. Put your weight down on your back truck as you start grinding.

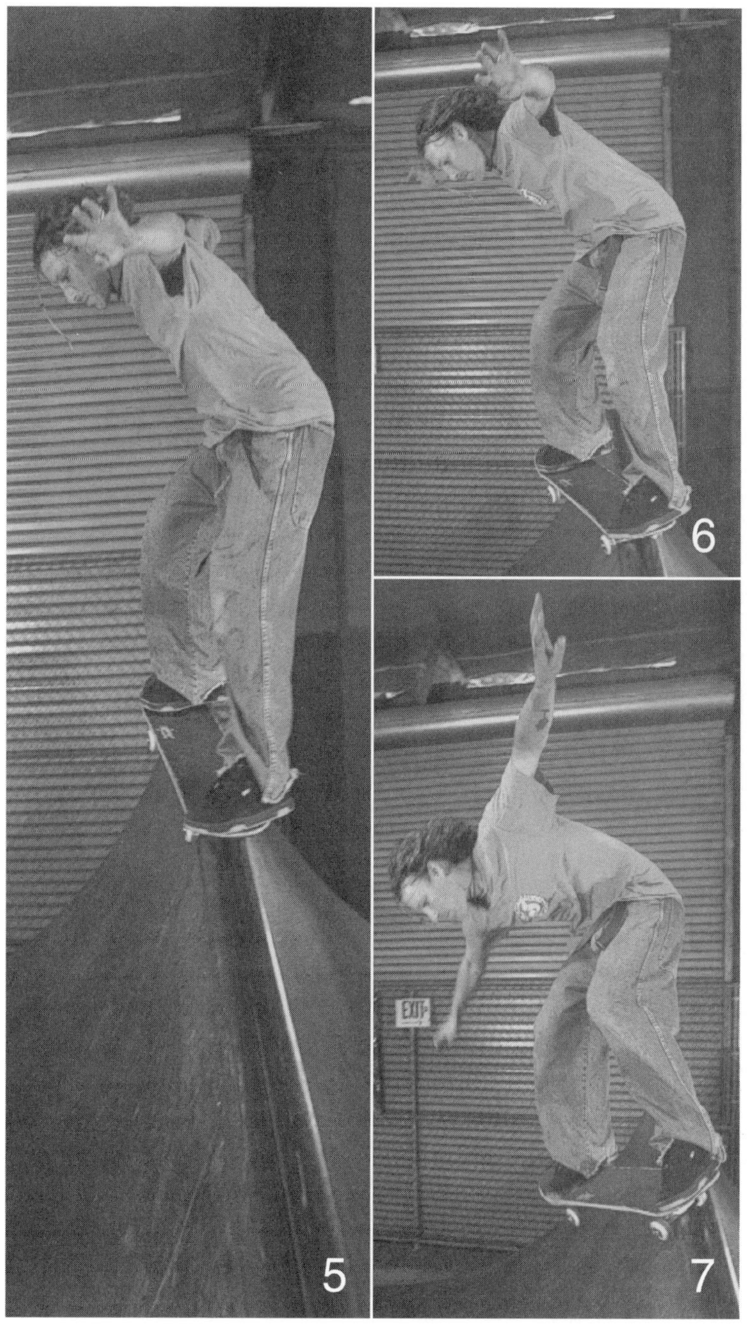
5
6
7
EXIT

Lean centered over the spine along the coping for full grind extension. When you start to feel the grind stopping, start leaning with your shoulders and head back on the other side of the ramp. Bring the nose around and lean forward riding straightforward. Throw your arms in the air and tell me you just don't care.

bigspin disaster over spine

Doug Werner

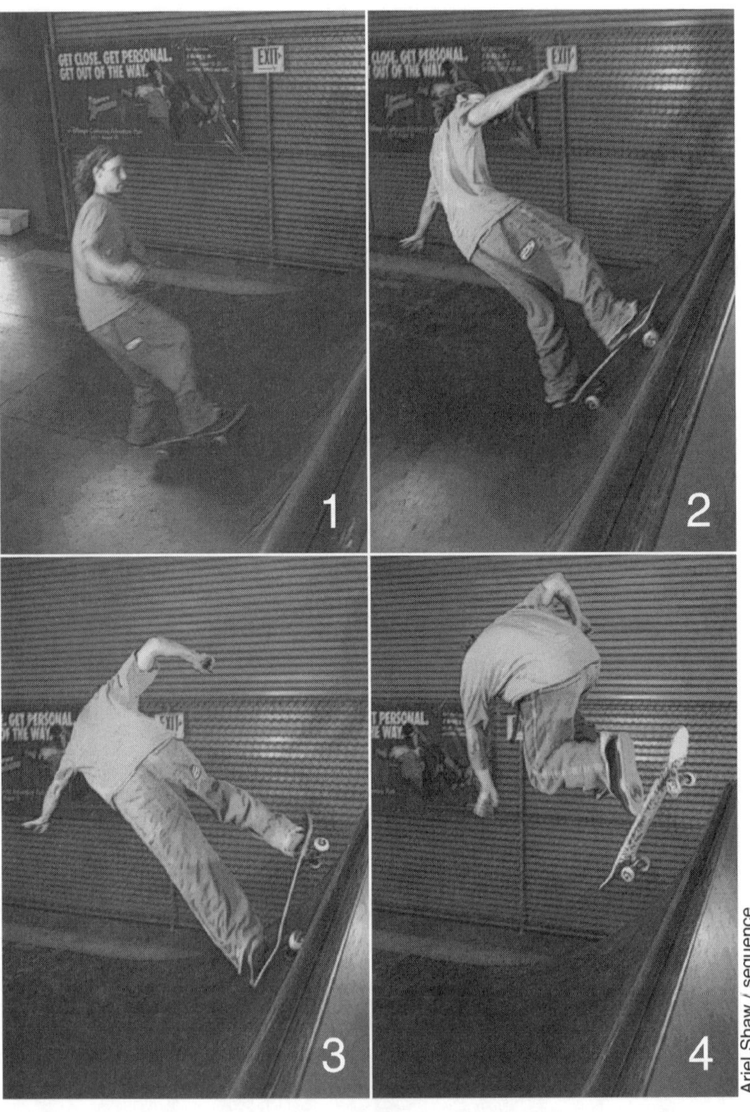

Ariel Shaw / sequence

After you learn bigspins on flat ground, take them to the spine ramp. This trick is so cool. You should try it on a ramp before you try it on a spine ramp. Ride straight up the tranny with a medium amount of speed. With your back foot, shuvit your board 360 by putting your back foot on the inside part of the tail to get full rotation out of the board. Shuvit the board 360 with your feet

while going backside. Try to get above the coping. You must trust yourself with your feet position because you have to catch the board in the air to land disaster on the spine. Turn your body 180, land disaster with your feet spread out over the bolts. Now the easy part, just lean your head and shoulders over the spine into the fakie position. Ride the board fakie. Try this trick again.

8
9
10

3

new school

rider: Brahyan Lopez

Steve Badillo

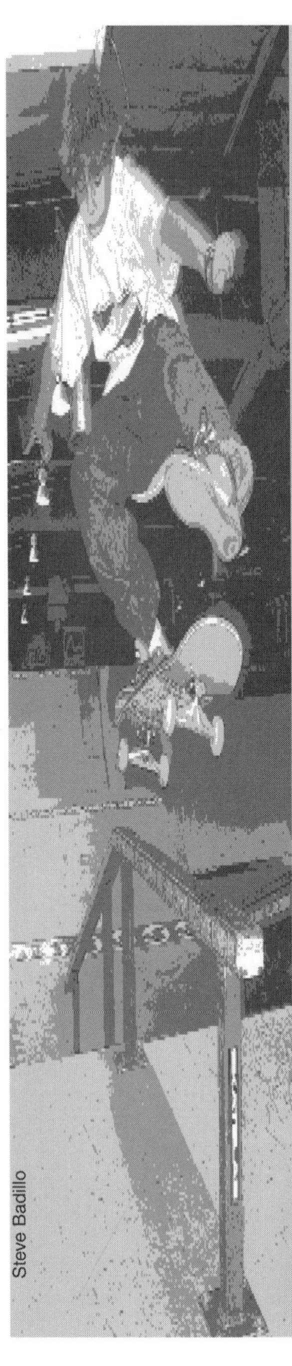
Steve Badillo

New school

New school for me began in 1990 when I was doing kickflips and boardsliding small handrails. Freestyle skateboarding was turning into street skating. Technical footwork was done with normal boards instead of freestyle boards. Kickflips, shuvits and boardsliding were the new generation of tricks kids were doing. In the mid '90s there was a big gap between old-school skaters and new-school skaters. I skated for Alva Skateboards at the time (and still do!) and traveled a lot with old-school legend Tony Alva. But I skated both new-school and old-school tricks and continue to do so today. To be well-rounded in skateboarding means to be adaptable to all terrains. The three other skateboarders in this section are consistent, fundamentally solid and creative in their skateboarding. It's always fun when I get to session with these guys. Thank you, Simon Corral, Brahyan Lopez and Torey Pudwill.

halfcab kickflip
Doug Werner

Doug Werner / sequence

This trick was shot at Silver Strand Beach where I live. SSL. With medium speed ride fakie with your feet in the kickflip position. Bend your knees and snap the tail as you do the 180 kickflip. Kick your front foot out to flip the board. Keep your knees bent and high in the air so the board can flip under your feet. Rotate your head and shoulders 180 with your feet spread out to

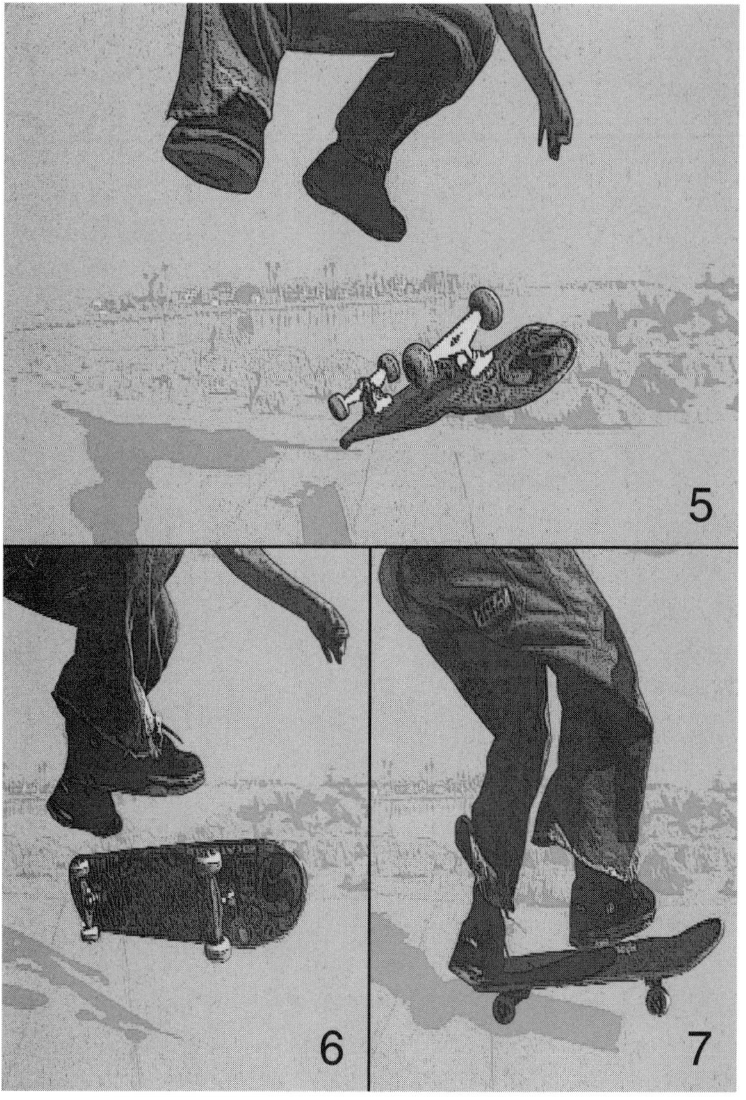

land on the bolts. Land on the board and don't feed the seagulls or wildcats.

8
9

fakie caballerial kickflip

Doug Werner

Ariel Shaw / sequence

This is the full 360 rotation from the halfcab flip. I finish the trick with an unintentional switch manuel. Start out going fakie with full but controllable speed. You are going to wind up throwing your arms and shoulders 360. First snap that ollie and kick out your front foot to do the 360 kickflip. Rotate your body 360 in the air above your board. Keep your knees bent and above the

5
6
7

board. Catch the board with your feet as you start to land fakie. Lean fakie as you land so you don't get thrown off the board. Don't get frustrated with this trick. Just practice and work on the full rotation.

SKATELAB
INDEPENDENT
8

pop shuvit

Doug Werner

Doug Werner / sequence

This is a fundamental flat ground trick that every skater should know. This trick can be done on almost any terrain. Skate at any speed and bend your knees as you snap the ollie. When you ollie, shuvit the tail with your tail foot backside. This means you push the tail around in the air. This should spin the board around 180. Use your front foot to guide the board around. Keep your

knees bent and above the board as you catch it with your feet. Land on top of the bolts and skate away. Now try frontside pop shuvit.

9

backside bigspin

Doug Werner

Doug Werner / sequence

I wanted to show the bigspin on flat ground so you could learn it before you took it to the spine ramp. Basically the bigspin is a 360 shuvit with a 180 body variel. Start by going forward with your back foot on the inside part of the tail and your front foot on the bolts. As you begin to 360 shuvit, push the tail to spin the board around. Get your knees up in the air above your board.

Start rotating your body 180 as you catch the board with your feet over the bolts. Lean fakie and ride it out. Now try it down some stairs.

8

backside kickflip disaster

Doug Werner

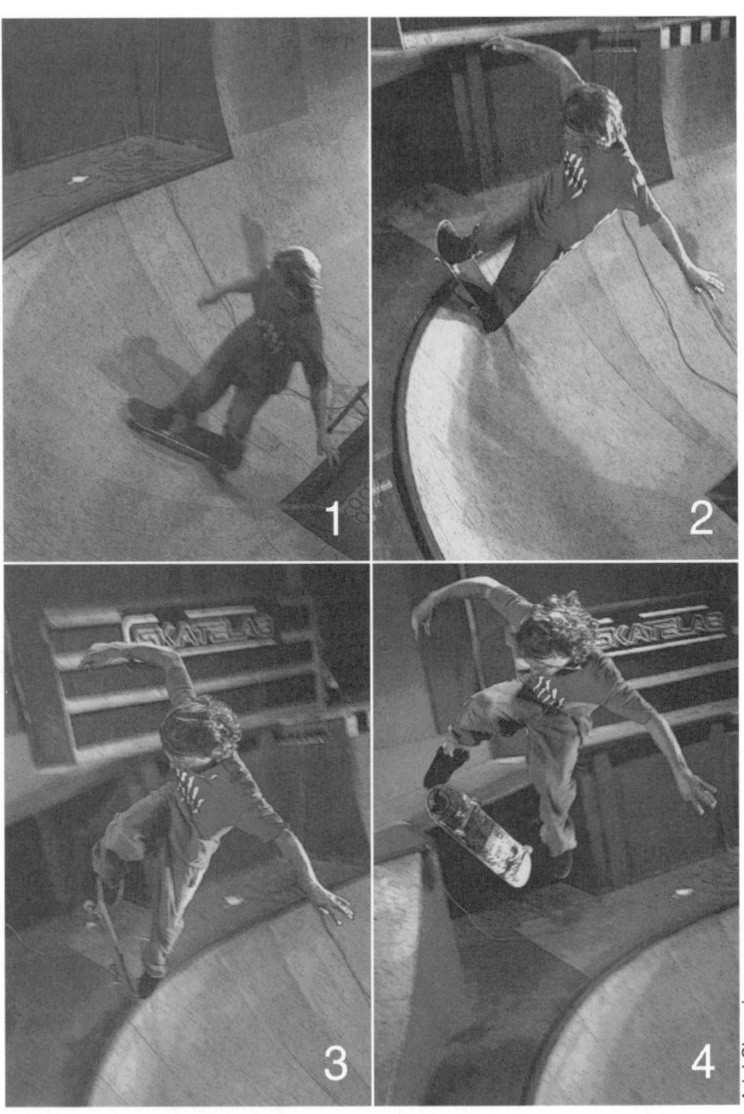

Ariel Shaw / sequence

Another one of my favorite tricks. It can be done on ramps, banks, pools and curbs. In this sequence I do it as a transfer from corner ramp to quarter pipe on the second level. The Skatelab ramps that hosted this trick are gone now but will always be remembered. This trick is on the cover of the book. You can do it going at about normal speed but for this sequence

I was going full speed to boardslide the disaster. As you approach the coping, have your feet in the kickflip position. Pop off the coping and kick your front foot up and out to flip the board. Once again keep your knees bent and over the board while it is rotating under you. Stay centered over the board as you catch it with your feet. Just as you catch the board, start

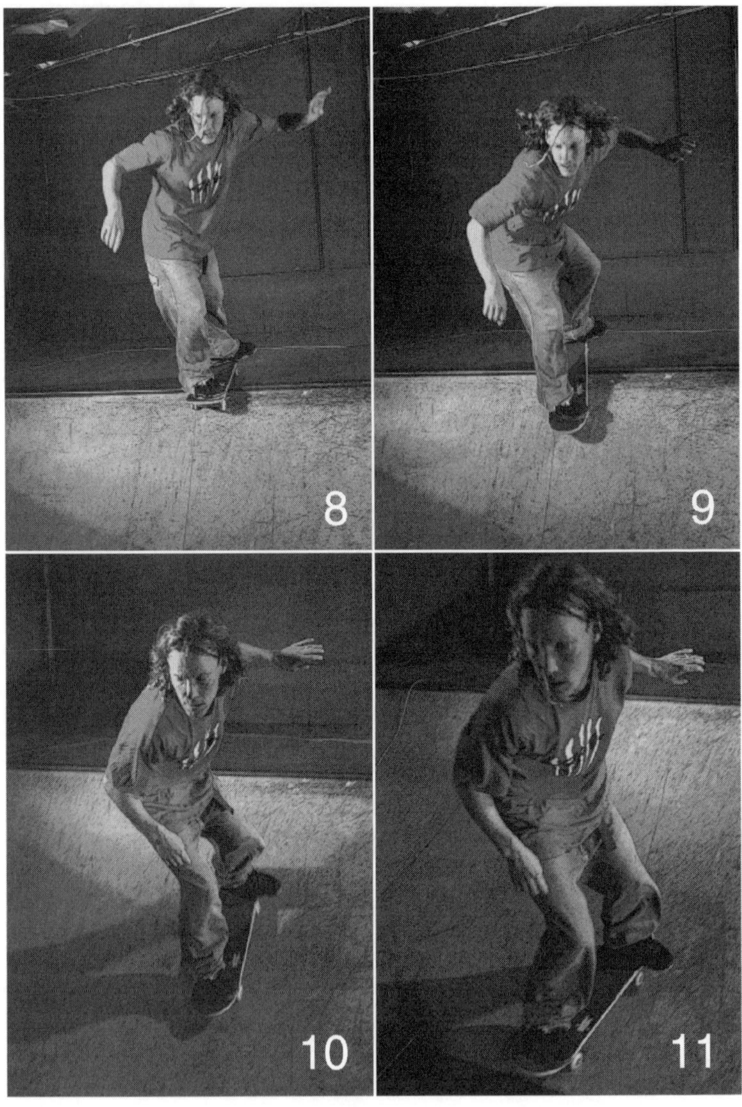

leaning into the transitions as you land disaster. Push your front foot down when you come in the tranny and clear the coping so you don't hang up on it. Lean forward and ride away feeling stoked.

benihana
MATIX
rider: Brahyan Lopez
Steve Badillo

Steve Badillo / sequence

I did this trick for the back cover of my first book *Skateboarder's Start Up*. Here Brahyan Lopez blasts a benihana over the volcano at Skatelab. Nice job. This trick can be done on ramps, banks and bowls. Start out going Mach 1 so you can clear the distance and pop your ollie high enough to kick out your back foot. Snap an ollie as you hit the lip. Right away start reaching

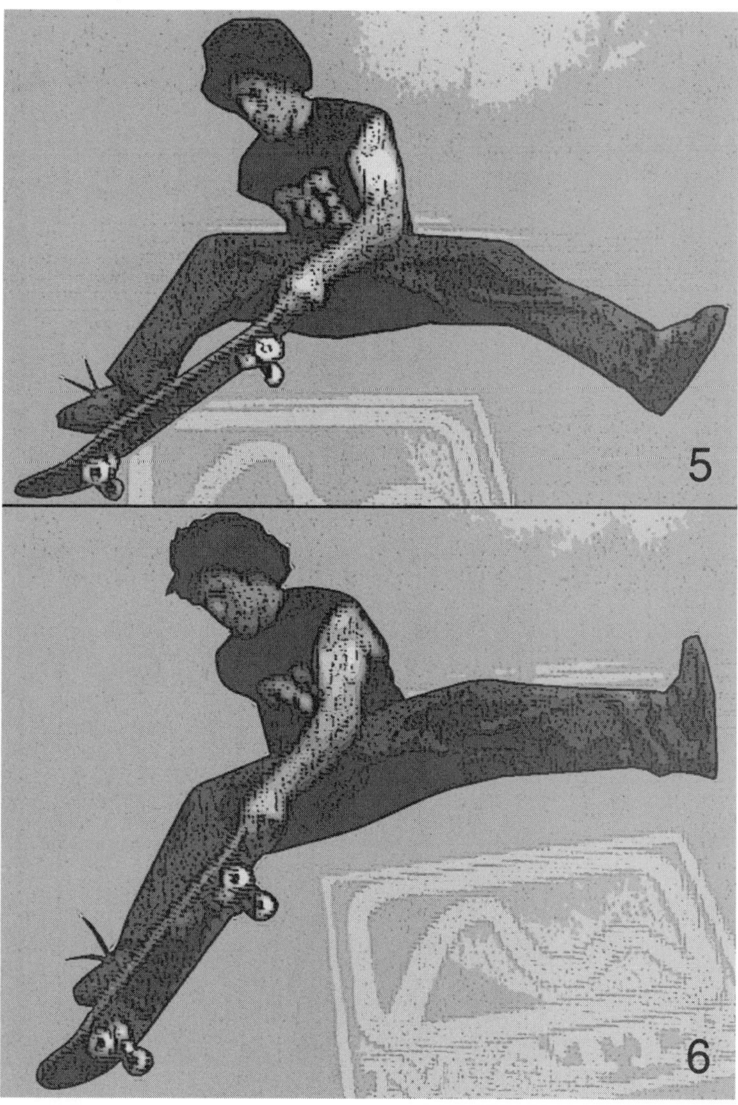

down with your trailing hand to grab the tail. As you do this, kick your back foot out and extend it as far as possible. Point your front foot forward for full extension. Lean forward as you land. Let go of the tail as you bring your tail foot back to the board. Stick the landing. Right on.

7
8
9

bluntslide

Mikey Pacheco

Mikey Pacheco / sequence

Bluntslides are fun and easy once you have them wired. They can be done on ramps, banks, ledges, handrails and curbs. Approach the lip with as much speed as you can. The faster you go the longer you will slide. Depending on the obstacle you are skating, you will have to ollie into the bluntslide, but I'm doing it on a bank, so I slide into it. Push down on the tail as you start to

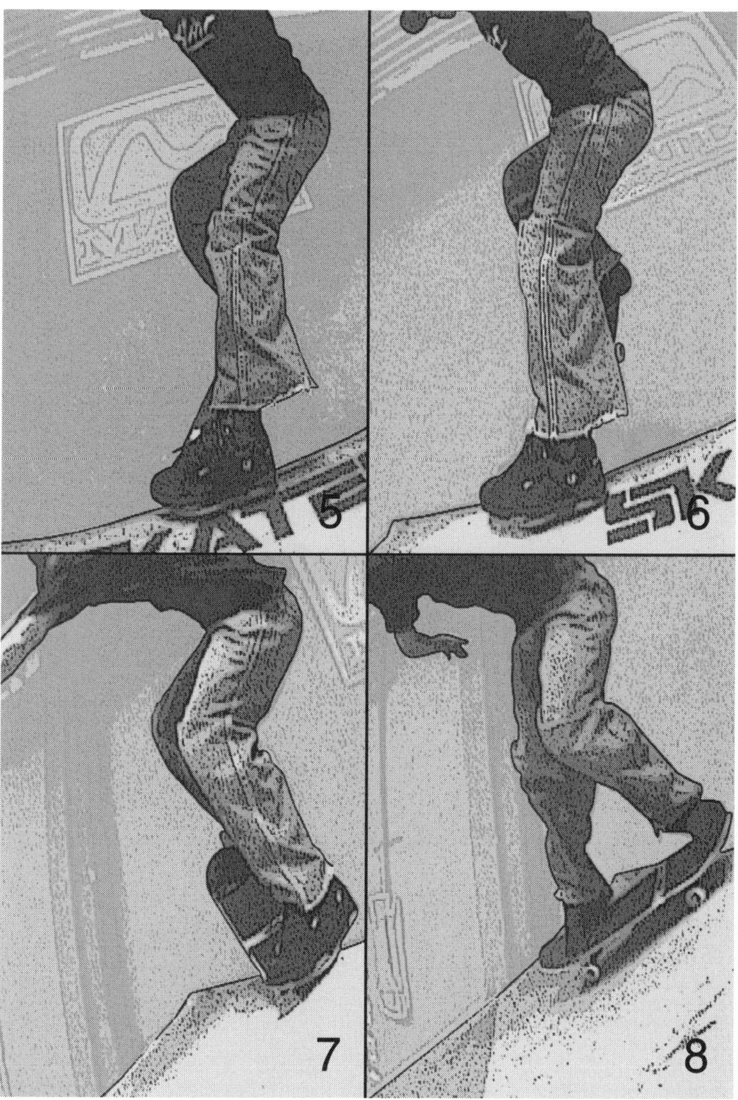

slide. Lean in on it with your body centered over the board. Your feet should be spread apart over the tail and front bolts. When you get to the end of the bank, swing the nose around and lean forward as you ride into the sunset.

9

Mikey Pacheco

Mikey Pacheco / sequence

This is a creative trick where you use a combination of other tricks to make one. You can do this trick on any ledge or curb. Get on your wooden toy and ride fast toward the ledge. You need enough speed to boardslide and grind. Snap an ollie and point your front foot up and over the ledge to get into a frontside boardslide. Slide a little and switch your body weight to the front

truck. Lift the back truck around to the ledge and put it on the lip. Now you should be in the switch 50-50 position. Start leaning switch to grind down the ledge and stay centered. As you get to the end of the ledge, lift the nose up (back truck) to clear the landing. Keep leaning switch and ride away. Now try it backside boardslide to switch frontside 50-50.

8
9
10

rider: Torey Pudwill

Steve Badillo

Steve Badillo / sequence

Handrail tricks are definitely new school. Here is my friend Torey Pudwill, a young ripper with a bright future. Approach the rail with medium speed. Snap an ollie and focus on locking the back truck with the rail in feeble position. Make sure you ollie high enough to get over the rail. Point the front truck over the rail and straighten out your front leg for style. Stay centered over your

board. Feeble grind down the rail. When you reach the end of the rail, lift up slightly with the nose so you can land it clean. Lean forward and ride away. Tea time, anyone?

8

kickflip 5-0 grind

rider: Torey Pudwill

Steve Badillo

This is another combination of a couple of tricks for one really cool one. Ride toward the rail backside with plenty of speed. Your feet should be in the kickflip position. Snap an ollie and kick your front foot up and out to flip your board. Make sure you ollie high enough to flip the board and get on top of the rail. Catch the board with your feet and spread them out over the bolts into the

Steve Badillo / sequence

5

5-0 grind. Keep the nose up as you grind through it. When you reach the end of the rail lean forward and land it clean.

6

8
COMPANY

9

backside lipslide

rider: Brahyan Lopez

Steve Badillo

Backside lipslides down handrails are so styley and should be in your bag of tricks. Approach the handrail going backside. Pop off the biggest ollie you can to get over the rail and to have enough speed to slide down. Bend your knees as you snap the ollie. Float over the rail, tweaking out the back truck and pointing the front truck backside. Your feet should be spread over the board. As you land on the rail, keep your back and waist twisted backside. Your head should be looking forward at the rail — this will keep you

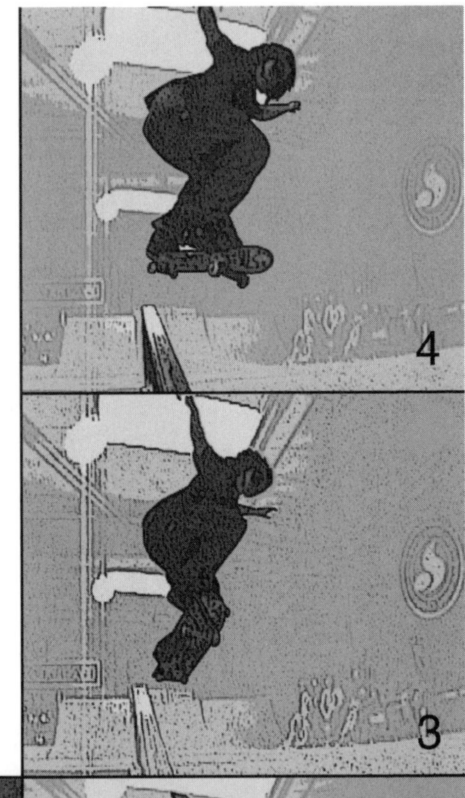

Steve Badillo / sequence

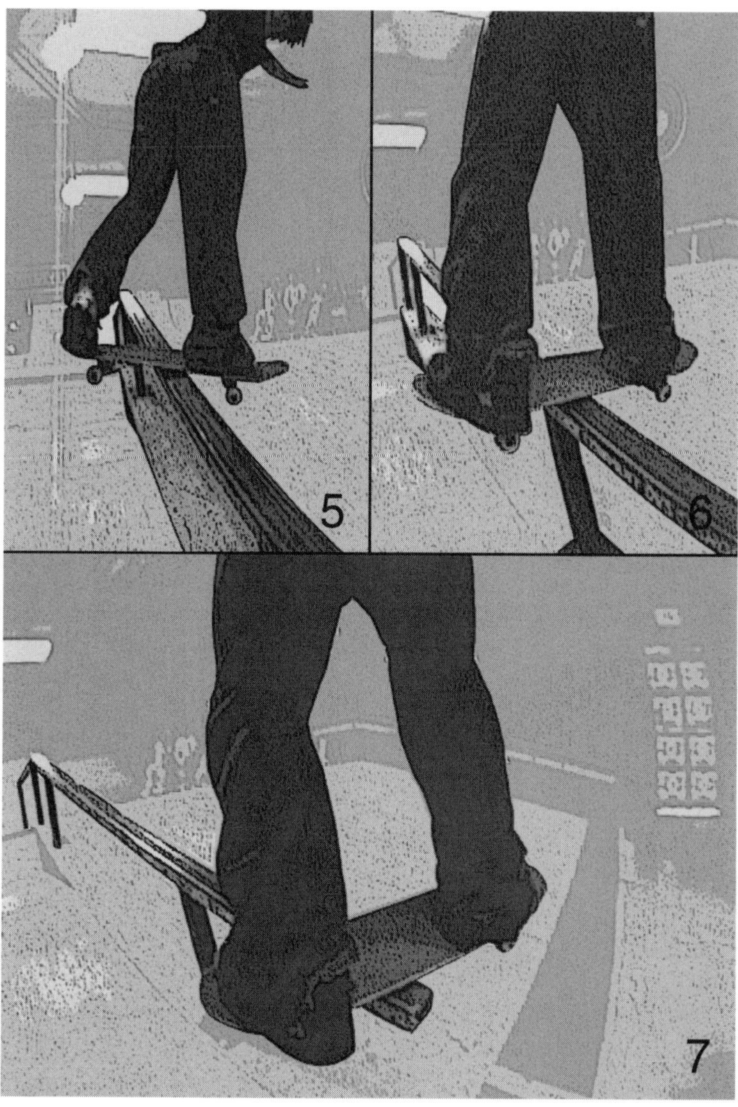

balanced while sliding down. If you don't twist your waist and keep your head looking forward, you will slip off the rail. When you reach the end of the handrail, bring your front truck around 90 degrees and lean forward. Do it again.

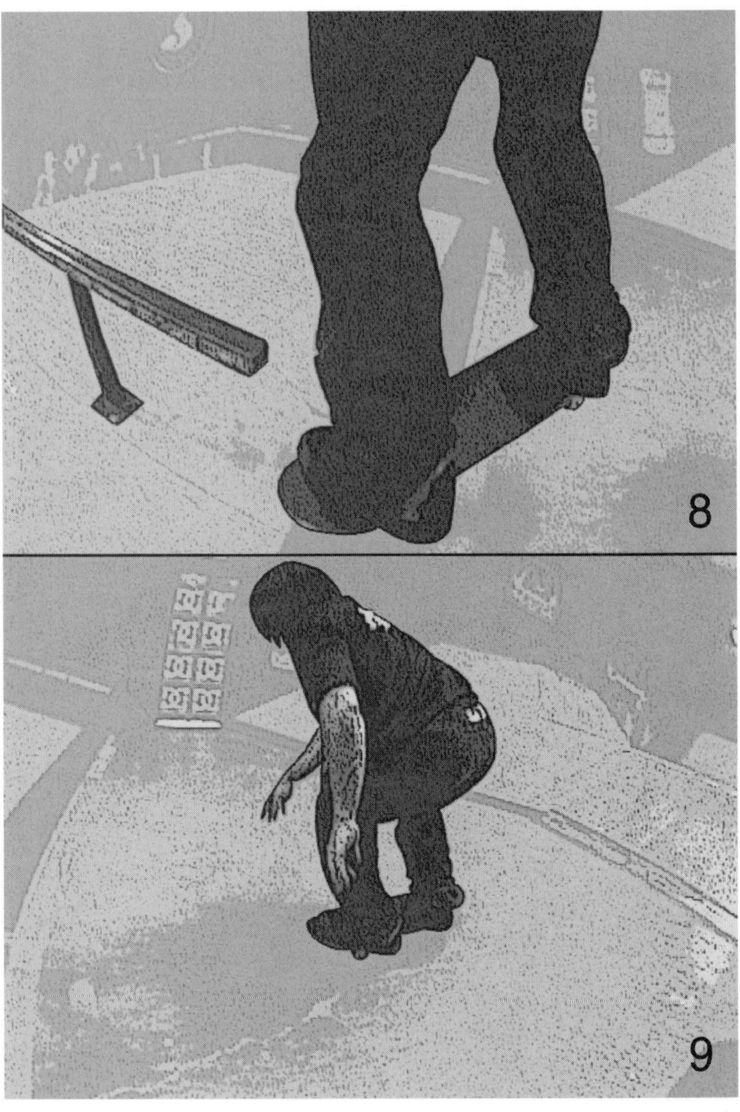
8
9

frontside 50-50

Doug Werner

Ariel Shaw / sequence

When you start learning to do handrails, frontside 50-50 should be one of the first tricks you try after you learn normal backside boardslides. Skate up to the handrail going frontside with medium speed. Hit the rail at a slight angle for a better ollie. Snap a big ollie and lean up and over the rail. Concentrate on getting both trucks locked onto the handrail. From there lean for-

ward as you start grinding your frontside 50-50. Your feet should be spread over the board. When you reach the end of the rail, lift the nose up to clear the landing. Lean forward and ride away.

8
9

rider: Simon Corral

Steve Badillo

Before learning switch crooked grinds on handrails, you should know how to switch ollie and how to do normal crooked grinds. Simon Corral is a technical wizard — especially on handrails and flat ground. Start by going switch with medium speed and hit the rail at a slight angle. Snap a switch ollie with your front truck up and at the rail. Concentrate on locking the front truck into the switch crooked position. Once you lock into switch crooked grind, put your weight on the front truck to

Steve Badillo / sequence

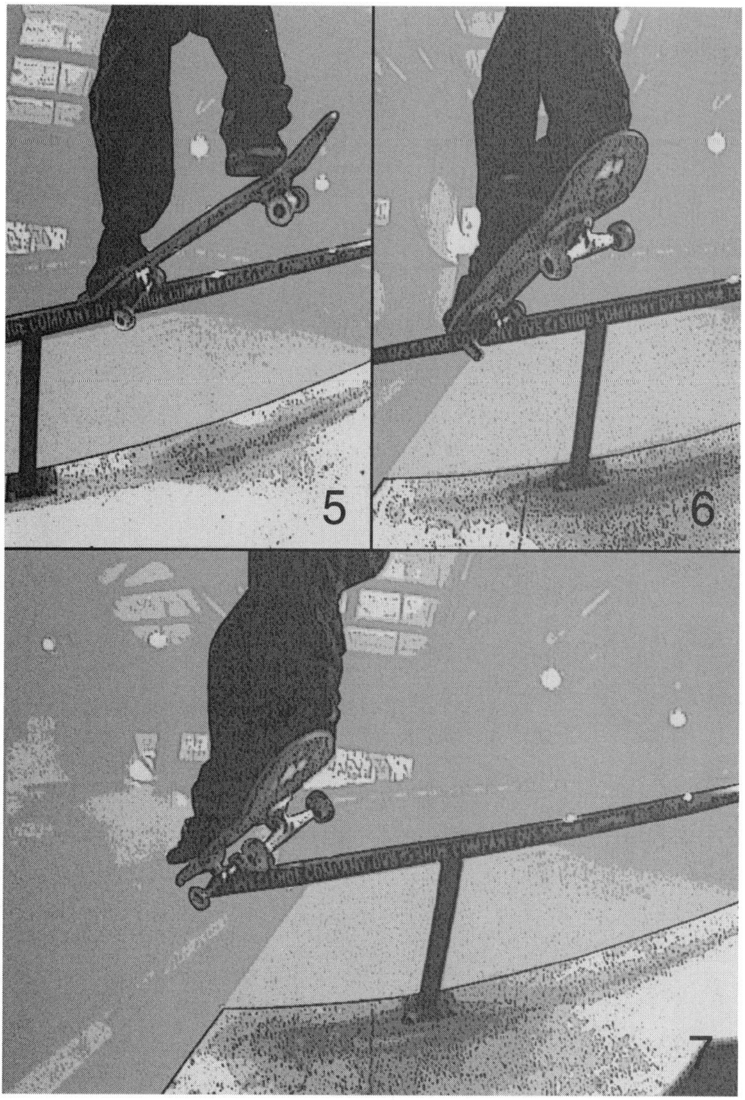

grind down the rail. Your feet should be spread over the board for balance. Almost at the end of the handrail, do a little switch nollie by shifting your weight to your back truck to lift the nose up. Land it and ride away switch.

8
9

frontside kickflip tailslide to fakie

rider: Simon Corral

Steve Badillo

The last trick in the book is the most technical on the handrail. Simon, it's all you. Approach the handrail frontside at a slight angle with medium speed. Your feet should be in the kickflip position. Snap your ollie and kick out your front foot to flip the board under your feet. Try to flip the tail toward the rail. Keep your knees bent and over the board. Stick your back foot on the tail on the rail. Put your weight on the tail and slide down the rail. That rhymes. Your front foot should be on the bolts and

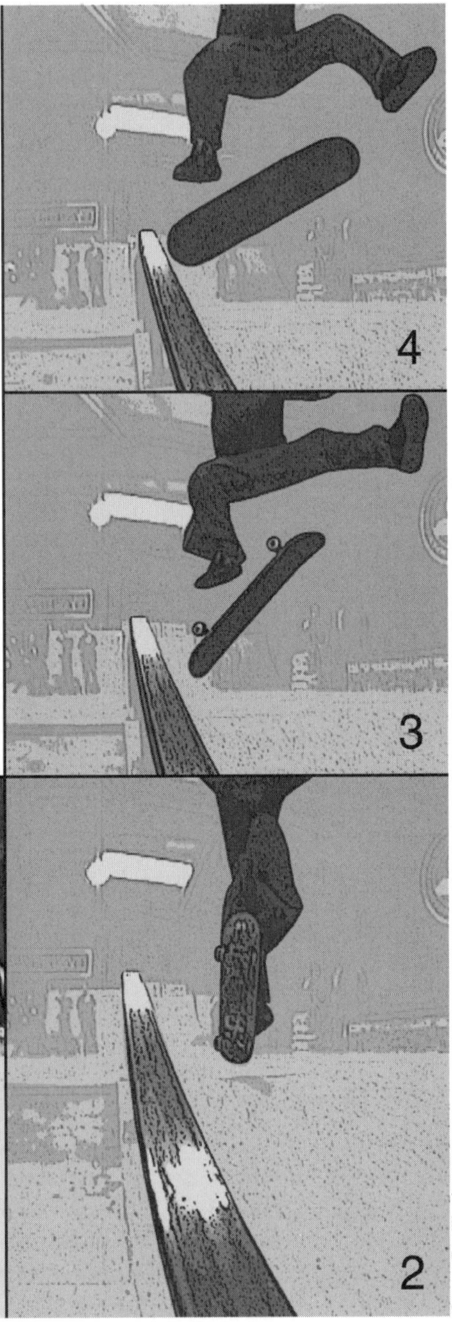

Steve Badillo / sequence

your back foot on the tail. When you approach the end of the rail, bring your tail foot around to fakie. This means you need to shift your body weight 90 degrees. Land fakie and lean forward. Next, pull down your pants.

8
9

4

old school
new school

photos by Ariel Shaw

Interview: Steve Badillo / July 2003

What do you want to say in this book?
What I want to get across to kids is the importance of being a well-rounded, adaptable skateboarder. What I mean by that is developing a solid foundation of tricks that includes New School, Old School and everything in between. An adaptable skateboarder is able to skate any terrain — pools, streets, skateparks, trannies, ramps, vertical ramps, ledges and rails.

> An adaptable skateboarder is able to skate any terrain ...

Skateboarders should develop both an adaptability to the terrain they will be skating and tricks to go with it. A lot of kids nowadays seem to be growing up learning one-sided. I like to teach young skaters to be well-rounded who can do everything.

Do you see kids getting stuck in a groove?
I see a lot of kids learning new-school stuff and being able to skate only certain terrains. When they go to terrains that they are not used to skating, they don't know what to do.

We should define terms. What is Old School and New School?
Old School refers to what the great skateboarding legends have done. Guys like Lance Mountain, Stevie Caballero, Tony Alva — these guys invented tricks many years ago. Over time their tricks have been developed by many other skaters into rad styles. The same old

tricks but with style. Old school refers to tricks that were done many years ago by the great skateboarding legends and can be done almost anywhere. New school involves more technical footwork — ollies and flips — that the new superstar skateboarders are doing.

Give an example of an old-school trick. Who invented the trick and how has it mutated over the years?
An old-school trick would be the boneless — frontside and backside boneless. It's very old school. I don't know who invented it, but it's been done by everyone. It's one of the tricks you can take to any terrain.

> When you see a skater able to merge both old school and new school and perform it anywhere, it inspires people. It inspires kids.

So it's a good basic trick to have in your quiver?
Definitely.

What are some new-school tricks?
Any of the flip tricks. You're talking 360 kickflips. Cab kickflips or heel flips or frontside flips or casper flips. Technical tricks.

Technical tricks involve flipping?
Technical is when you're using your feet. When you're using the ollie and you go past the ollie — you flip the board around, you spin the board around and you're able to do it on ledges, rails, coping, lips and banks. It

takes a lot of practice and your footwork has to be really on. You gotta work your ollies and your footwork when you're doing technical tricks.

So a great skater is someone who can merge old school and new school?
The great skaters that are out there — the superstars of today — they bust out old-school tricks, bust out new-school tricks, and they can bust out in any terrain. When you see a skater like Lance Mountain — he is an old-school guy, skates great with great style — he can bust out any old-school trick in the book. But he combines street skating, which he has adapted to his style. He can do kickflips, nose grinds and K grinds. He can do handrails and ledges. When you see someone like that, it's inspiring. When you see a skater able to merge both old school and new school and perform anywhere, it inspires people. It inspires kids.

For young people coming up who have become good skaters ... what is the next thing that he or she looks for? Sponsorship?
I think so. Once they develop the skills to skate different terrains and have a small bag of tricks going, they want to start looking for sponsorship to help progress their skateboarding career.

A sponsor being ...
A board sponsor, a truck sponsor, a wheel sponsor, a clothes sponsor. It helps skaters financially and it helps them out in their skating career if they choose to go in that direction. Skateboarding to a lot of kids is just having fun and doing it for yourself. But kids that have talent and want to make money at it and make it a

So, definitely the person's attitude, his ability and his adaptability to terrain will attract sponsors.

career, have some options to think about. Companies looking to sponsor kids want marketability and attitude — how they portray themselves, how they dress, how they look — along with their skating abilities. And the companies that are stoked on those kind of skateboarders are actually looking for kids who can skate everything — not just handrails and ledges, but skateparks and trannies — transitions, vertical ramps and pools. A young, talented skater who's skating everything and is well-rounded gets the sponsors stoked. And his or her marketability. An attitude, whether positive or negative, does attract certain sponsors. So, definitely the person's attitude, his ability and his adaptability to terrain will attract sponsors.

You can have a negative attitude and there are sponsors who like that bad boy type of thing?
That's very popular in skateboarding, the bad boy skateboarder. Many skate companies sponsor bad boy skateboarders.

The bad boy still needs to show up when he is supposed to — right? (laughter)
They don't always show up, but I know that different trends in skateboarding sell and those trends have to do with the attitudes of pro skateboarders. And the marketability of those pro skateboarders. Companies

Realistically, a pro skater needs to be able to do a lot of different things to make money.

look for that and then they try to exploit it, they try to make money at it. It goes both ways. It's a positive and a negative thing in skateboarding.

Picking up on that thread, you have a career in skateboarding. You make a living through instruction, you have a summer camp, you give private lessons, you model and act in commercials and in music videos and car commercials. You're on TV. What advice would you give skaters who want to make it a career? Are there specific stepping stones? Is gaining sponsorship the first thing to do?

The first thing to do is develop skills and the kind of skateboarding you want to do. Then try to attract different sponsors with your skating ability. But keep in mind that despite how popular skateboarding is today, there's not a lot of room for pros to make much money at it. Only the top 20 pros are making really good money. All the other pros in the business are making OK money, just enough to pay bills and sometimes not even that. So it's really up to the individual and the path he seeks in skateboarding.

Realistically, a pro skater needs to be able to do a lot of different things to make money. Like you said, I run a skateboard camp and give skateboard lessons, I have written skateboard books, I do TV, judge contests, enter contests, tour, do demos and earn money from board sales. I mean, for pro skaters to be out there making money, they have to work at it, they have to hustle, and they have to do many different things in skateboarding. You know, there are only a few Tony Hawks who can make the big money out there. But even Tony Hawk does a lot of different things in skateboarding. So to be a skateboarder, you gotta love it, you gotta live it, you gotta breath it, you gotta eat it. You have to be a skateboarder.

And you have to make sacrifices to be able to make enough money to live on. What I mean by sacrifices is that you have to do many things that you wouldn't necessarily think pro skateboarders do. For example, I go to places like the Boys and Girls Club in different cities and talk to kids about skateboarding and try to encourage them. The best thing skateboarders can do for skateboarding, as a general idea and goal, is to perpetuate skateboarding itself. If you can be a positive force in skateboarding and are able to perpetuate the skateboarding world, then you will find different avenues to be successful and to satisfy your own goals. Like I said, all those guys that invented tricks were expanding skateboarding. As well as those guys who tour bringing skateboarding to new parts of the United States and the world, those guys that build skateparks and push to get skateparks in different cities. And skateboarding instruction in skate camps and skate schools. All these things are positive goals to help make skateboarding bigger, broader and accessible to more and more kids.

Talking to kids and encouraging their skateboarding. Just hanging at Silver Strand with the neighbors.

Doug Werner

> The best thing skateboarders can do for skateboarding, as a general idea and goal, is to perpetuate skateboarding itself.

Well said. Just before a trick, you appear to have a ritual ...
Breathing and visualizing the trick helps me mentally to get through the trick. To recognize what it feels like to land it. You have to visualize what it feels like to successfully land and to ride it away. It's easy to do the trick halfway and bail out every time. You have to visualize the landing part so you can ride it out. If you can visualize the feeling of the whole trick, including the landing part, it makes it easier to consistently execute the trick. When you do big stunts, breathing helps calm your heart and focus your mind. Just breath and visualize and get the juices flowing. It gets me and my mind set and it gets me to focus ... gets my energies focused on that particular trick. And like I was saying, I visualize the landing so that I can pull the trick ...

Not just the hero part ...
Not just the hero part! The hero part is easy to do. I mean, it's easy to fling yourself up and do a flip and bail out of it. It's all about the landing. It's all about visualizing the landing and completing the whole trick.

We have talked about how skaters and tricks have been evolving. Have you noticed how skateboarding gear has been evolving? In the history

of skateboarding there are some major breakthroughs. For example, you have the introduction of urethane wheels back in 1975. Have you noticed anything — can you comment on anything in the last couple of years?

> The hero part is easy to do. I mean, it's easy to fling yourself up and do a flip and bail out of it. It's all about the landing.

When I was a kid in the '80s, there were a lot of different skateboard designs and shapes. Each pro skateboarder back in the '80s had his own unique shape. It was really cool at the time. Since then the skateboard actually has been simplified. It's symmetrical now. The nose and tail are the same — well-rounded. No more steep-ass tri-tail with Aaron Murray bumps on the side for flair. Board shapes have been simplified and are more uniform except for the graphics. When kids go out and buy boards, they buy the board that fits them, but you know, they are almost all the same.

Different sizes?
There are different sizes — minis, longboards — but it's come to a point where the graphics are more important to kids than the shape.

Sounds like board design has been perfected, at least up to this point in time.
Sure.

Trucks?
Trucks will get lighter, but the basic design of trucks hasn't changed much.

Wheels?
Just different sized wheels for different terrains. Bigger wheels on bigger ramps, pools, big halfpipes. For street skateboarding — skating ledges and rails, for ollies and gaps — you use smaller wheels for lightness and better reaction time — to rotate the board faster.

I see skateboard manufacturers dealing with new materials and new ideas, but basically today's skateboard design is where it's at, and I don't see it changing that much in the future.

What will keep evolving is what the skater is doing on that skateboard. The old-school skateboarders gave us the foundation — the basic tricks. The superstars of today are using those tricks, inventing new ones and taking them to the extreme. I mean, grinding down 20-stair handrails, doing a long ledge ... they are taking the same old tricks and new tricks and actually pushing them to the very, very,

The old-school skateboarders gave us the foundation — the basic tricks. The superstars of today are using those tricks, inventing new ones and taking them to the extreme.

Mikey Pacheco

very extreme ... blasting the longer airs, grinding the longest grinds and sliding the longest ledges.

Resources

In alphabetical order we have a healthy dose of info about skateboarding as it relates to:

Books
Camps
Magazines
Museums
Organizations
Public skateparks (building of)
Shops
Skateparks (finding one)
Television
Web sites
Videos

For a quick fix go to **www.skateboarding.com** — this is an informative (but not the only) portal into the skateboarding galaxy. For face-to-face, find a real skateboard shop and talk to real skaters.

Books
Books discovered on **amazon.com** and **barnesandnoble.com**.

Baccigaluppi, John. *Declaration of Independents*. San Francisco, California: Chronicle Books, 2001.

Bermudez, Ben. *Skate! The Mongo's Guide to Skateboarding*. New York, New York: Cheapskate Press, 2001.

Borden, Ian. *Skateboarding, Space and the City.* New York, New York: Berg, 2001.

Brooke, Michael. *The Concrete Wave: The History of Skateboarding.* Toronto, Ontario: Warwick Publishing, 1999.

Burke, L.M. *Skateboarding! Surf the Pavement.* New York, New York: Rosen Publishing Group, Inc., 1999.

Davis, James. *Skateboard Roadmap.* England: Carlton Books Limited, 1999.

Gould, Marilyn. *Skateboarding.* Mankato, Minnesota: Capstone Press, 1991.

Gutman, Bill. *Skateboarding: To the Extreme.* New York, New York: Tom Doherty Associates, Inc., 1997.

Hawk, Tony. *Hawk*. New York, New York: Regan Books, 2001.

Powell, Ben. *Extreme Sports: Skateboarding.* Hauppauge, New York: Barron's Educational Series, Inc. 1999.

Riggins, Edward. *Ramp Plans*. San Francisco, California: High Speed Productions, 2000.

Ryan, Pat. *Extreme Skateboarding.* Mankato, Minnesota: Capstone Press, 1998.

Shoemaker, Joel. *Skateboarding Streetstyle.* Mankato, Minnesota: Capstone Press, 1995.

Thrasher. *Insane Terrain.* New York, New York: Universe Publishing, 2001.

Camps

Donny Barley Skate Camp
1747 West Main Road
Middletown, Rhode Island 02842
401-848-8078

Lake Owen
HC 60 Box 60
Cable, Wisconsin 54821
715-798-3785

Magdalena Ecke Family YMCA
200 Saxony Road
Encinitas, California 92023-0907
760-942-9622

Mission Valley YMCA
5505 Friars Road
San Diego, California 92110
619-298-3576

Skatelab
Steve Badillo Skate Camp
4226 Valley Fair Street
Simi Valley, California 93063
805-578-0040
vtaskate@aol.com

Snow Valley
PO Box 2337
Running Springs, California 92382
909-867-2751

Visalia YMCA
Sequoia Lake, California
211 West Tulare Avenue
Visalia, California 93277
559-627-0700

Woodward Camp
Box 93
Route 45
Woodward, Pennsylvania 16882
814-349-5633

Young Life Skate Camp
Hope, British Columbia, Canada
604-807-3718

Magazines

Big Brother
www.bigbrothermagazine.com

Skateboarder
Surfer Publications
PO Box 1028
Dana Point, California 92629

Thrasher
High Speed Productions
1303 Underwood Avenue
San Francisco, California 94124
415-822-3083
www.thrashermagazine.com

Transworld Skateboarding
353 Airport Road
Oceanside, California 92054

760-722-7777
www.skateboarding.com

Museums
Huntington Beach International Skate and Surf Museum
411 Olive Street
Huntington Beach, California
714-960-3483

Skatelab
4226 Valley Fair
Simi Valley, California
805-578-0040
www.skatelab.com

Skatopia
34961 Hutton Road
Rutland, Ohio 45775
740-742-1110

Organizations, movers, shakers . . .
Action Sports Retailer
Organizer of the Action Sports Retailer Trade Expos
949-376-8144
www.asrbiz.com

California Amateur Skateboard League (CASL) and PSL
Amateur and professional contest organizer
909-883-6176
Fax 909-883-8036

The Canadian Cup
416-960-2222

Extreme Downhill International
1666 Garnet Avenue #308
San Diego, California 92109
619-272-3095

International Association of Skateboard Companies (IASC)
PO Box 37
Santa Barbara, California 93116
805-683-5676
Fax 805-967-7537
iascsk8@aol.com
www.skateboardiasc.org

International Network for Flatland Freestyle Skateboarding
Abbedissavagen 15
746 95 Balsta, Sweden

KC Projects
Canadian amateur contest organizer
514-806-7838
kc_projects@aol.com
5148067838@fido.ca

National Amateur Skateboard Championships
Damn Am Series
National amateur contest organizer
813-621-6793
www.skateparkoftampa.com
www.nascseries.com

National Skateboarders Association of Australia (NSAA)
Amateur and professional contest organizers
61-2-9878-3876
www.skateboard.asn.au

The Next Cup
Southern California amateur contest organizer
858-874-4970 ext. 114 or 129
www.thenextcup.com

Real Amateur Skateboarding
Amateur contest organizer
619-501-1341
realamateurskateboarding@hotmail.com

Skateboarding Association of America
Amateur contest organizer
727-523-0875
www.skateboardassn.org

Skatepark Association of the USA (SPAUSA)
Resource for skatepark planning/operating
310-823-9228
www.spausa.org

Southwest Sizzler
Southwestern amateur contest organizer
918-638-6492

Surf Expo
East Coast trade show
800-947-SURF
www.surfexpo.com

United Skateboarding Association (USA)
Skate event organizer and action sport marketing/promotions
732-432-5400 ext. 2168 and 2169
www.unitedskate.com

Vans Shoes
Organizer of the Triple Crown skate events
562-565-8267
www.vans.com

World Cup Skateboarding
Organizer of some of skating's largest events
530-888-0596
Fax 530-888-0296
danielle@wcsk8.com
www.wcsk8.com

Zeal Skateboarding Association
Southern California amateur contest organizer
909-265-3420
www.zealsk8.com

Public skateparks / information about building and starting up

Consolidated Skateboards
(see *The Plan*)
www.consolidatedskateboard.com

International Association of Skateboard Companies (IASC)
PO Box 37
Santa Barbara, California 93116
805-683-5676
Fax 805-967-7537
iascsk8@aol.com
www.skateboardiasc.org

Skatepark Association of the USA (SPAUSA)
310-823-9228
www.spausa.org

www.skatepark.org

Public skatepark designers / builders

Airspeed Skateparks LLC
2006 Highway 101 #154
Florence, Oregon 97439
503-791-4674
airspeed@airspeedskateparks .com
www.airspeedskateparks.com

CA Skateparks, Design/Build and General Contracting
273 North Benson Avenue
Upland, California 91786
562-208-4646
www.skatedesign.com

Dreamland Skateparks, Grindline Inc.
4056 23rd Avenue SW
Seattle, Washington 98106
206-933-7915
www.grindline.com

John Woodstock Designs
561-743-5963
johnwoodstock@msn.com
www.woodstockskateparks.com

Ramptech
www.ramptech.com

SITE Design Group, Inc.
414 South Mill Avenue, Suite 210
Tempe, Arizona 85281
480-894-6797
Fax 480-894-6792
mm@sitedesigngroup.com
www.sitedesigngroup.com

Spectrum Skatepark Creations, Ltd.
M/A 2856 Clifftop Lane, Whistler, B.C.
V0N 1B2 Canada
250-238-0140
design@spectrum-sk8.com
www.spectrum-sk8.com

Team Pain
864 Gazelle Trail
Winter Springs, Florida 32708
407-695-8215
tim@teampain.com
www.teampain.com

Shops / finding one close to you

Two (among quite a few) that will help:
www.skateboarding.com
www.skateboards.org

Skateparks / finding one close to you

Two (among quite a few) that will help:
www.skateboarding.com
www.skateboards.org

Television

ESPN

X Games
espn.go.com/extreme

NBC
Gravity Games
www.gravitygames.com

Web sites
www.board-trac.com
Market researchers for skateboarding industry.

www.bigbrother.com
A comprehensive site by *Big Brother* magazine.

www.exploratorium.edu/skateboarding
Glossary, scientific explanations and equipment for skating.

www.interlog.com/~mbrooke/skategeezer.html
International Longboarder magazine.

www.ncdsa.com
Northern California Downhill Skateboarding Association.

www.skateboardiasc.org
International Association of Skateboard Companies (IASC) is one of the leading advocates of skateboarding progress and provides a wealth of information.

www.skateboard.com
Chat and messages.
www.skateboarding.com
Every skater's site by *Transworld Skateboarding* magazine.

www.skateboards.org
Find parks, shops and companies here.

www.skatelab.com
One of Los Angeles area's largest indoor parks and world's largest skateboard museum.

www.skater.net
Skate parks and ramp plans.

www.smithgrind.com
Skate news wire

www.switchmagazine.com
Switch Skateboarding Magazine

www.thrashermagazine.com
A comprehensive site by *Thrasher* magazine.

More web sites
www.stevebadillo.com
www.stevebadillo@adelphia.net
www.skatelab.com
www.bokasmo.com
www.dvsshoes.com
www.teampain.com
www.rcmcsk8parks.com
www.alvaskates.com
www.gourethane.com

Videos / Instructional

411 Video Productions. *The First Step.*

411 Video Productions. *The Next Step.*

Hawk, Tony. *Tony Hawk's Trick Tips Volume I: Skateboarding Basics.* 900 Films, 2001.

Hawk, Tony. *Tony Hawk's Trick Tips Volume II: Essentials of Street.* 900 Films, 2001.

Thrasher Magazine. *How to Skateboard.* San Francisco, California: High Speed Productions, Inc., 1995.

Thrasher Magazine. *How to Skateboard Better.* San Francisco, California: High Speed Productions, Inc., 1997.

Transworld Skateboarding. *Starting Point.* Oceanside, California, 1997.

Transworld Skateboarding. *Trick Tips with Wily Santos.* Oceanside, California, 1998.

Transworld Skateboarding. *Starting Point Number Two.* Oceanside, California, 1999.

More addresses

Alva Skateboards
403-B Wisconsin Ave.
Oceanside, California 92054

Bokasmo
2141-K El Camino Real
Oceanside, California 92054

Geometric Construction
2420 Industry Street
Suite C
Oceanside, California 92054
760-721-6798

Go Urethane Wheel Company
15221 Transistor Lane
Huntington Beach, California
92649

Skatelab
4226 Valley Fair St.
Simi Valley, California 93063

Index

About the author

Mikey Pacheco

Steve Badillo

Steve Badillo is a professional skateboarder and skating coach. He has skated on MTV and in numerous ads and videos including those of Limp Bizkit, Offspring and The Donnas. He coaches at Skatelab in Simi Valley, California and lives with his wife Becca and son Gavin in nearby Silver Strand Beach. Steve's previous skate books are *Skateboarder's Start-Up* and *Skateboarding: New Levels* (Tracks Publishing).

www.stevebadillo.com